MW00711254

Morning Roses

To Colby
From Mike

Good Bless,

E. Pittman

Morning Roses

(Love Is Like That, Don'tcha Know)

C. E. Pittman

VANTAGE PRESS
New York

FIRST EDITION

Copyright © 1996 by C. E. Pittman

Published by Vantage Press, Inc.
516 West 34th Street, New York, New York 10001

Manufactured in the United States of America
ISBN: 0-533-11709-7

Library of Congress Catalog Card No.: 95-90782

0 9 8 7 6 5 4 3 2 1

To profess God's presence
among men today

Preface

Sometimes people go through life never knowing what special things they have. But not Ellie and me. We always knew. We knew on the first date, on the day the angels came for her, and on all the days in between.

Sometimes people go through life living only in regret. I was fortunate to go through life in an almost constant fog of love that surrounded me. The only regret I have is that Ellie and I can no longer dance in our kitchen at night.

I was an athletic senior and she was the school sweetheart when we met. Somehow, with a love for God and for each other, we managed to make it through the hard times, raise our children, and watch our grandchildren come into the world.

We danced nearly every day and laughter was always present. When Ellie became ill, people told me to let others take care of her.

Instead, I fed her and cared for her until she left on angels' wings. It was never a burden to me. She was my life. Love is like that, don'tcha know.

And if you didn't you're about to find out, because here is my story.

Ellie and I were the stars of life; whatever beauty we possessed was from one another!

God saw to that and love was sweet, don'tcha know?

Morning Roses

1

I was born April 14, 1919, in the small lead and zinc mining town of Oronogo, Missouri. In the early 1920s, Blue Flint miners were tough. The tougher a miner thought he was, the louder the miner would clog his boots on the board sidewalks.

Saloons were open game and fist fights occurred every night, just to prove who was the best man. Many times, when the fighting was over, the one left standing would help the loser up to his feet, and arm in arm, they would saunter back to the bar for another round.

This isn't true today in the 1990s. Minds have turned so violent that instead of fists it is now knives and guns and whatever else it takes to subdue the foe.

Why can't we as people understand that the most precious thing in the world is life? God have mercy.

The town blacksmith shop and sorghum mill was just down the back alley from our house. Uncle Bill Allen owned the blacksmith shop and sorghum mill. As far as I know, he never had a wife. I suppose he was about fifty years old at this time. This stern but sweet old man would let the neighborhood kids watch him do his blacksmithing at the forge. It was so fascinating to see him pound the red-hot metal into various shapes, such as horseshoes.

When sugarcane harvesttime came, Uncle Bill Allen would let us kids in the neighborhood watch the old mule go round and round while sugarcane stalks were fed into the mule-driven press, which squeezed out the sugarcane juice, which was then poured into a six-by-four-by-one-foot vat heated by an open-pit wood fire.

The special sweet smell from cooking of the cane juice filled the air, which told all the town folks and the families of these hard

1

rock miners that it was time to bring their pails for sorghum molasses, which made delicious gingerbread cakes. When these old miners came home for dinner, they were treated to the really special dessert topped with real homemade whipped cream. Wow! I can smell it now. As the soaking vat was emptied, Uncle Bill Allen would cut short pieces of cane stalk on a thirty-degree angle and let each of us kids push these sticks along the bottom of the vat. The molasses would curl up the stick. We would eat and eat until our stomachs would hurt. How sweet this once-a-year special treat was!

I was unaware that God's plan for my life was just beginning to take shape, even protecting me from death while I was trying to save my sister from a deadly whirlpool while swimming in Spring River near Alba, Missouri. With the help of my father, Roy T. Pittman, the rescue was accomplished.

Of course, this was just the beginning of miracles in God's plan for this nine-year-old country boy. Like most young boys at that time, my love for family and sports dominated my leisure summertime away from school classrooms. I loved to hear the old-timers speak of Bonnie and Clyde, who robbed the Oronogo Bank about that time. They shot up the town pretty good, and there are still bullet holes in some of the old building drainpipes as a reminder that these gangsters had been here. Luckily, no one was hurt.

However, this country boy's joy for the beautiful love song music floating out of the horn of an old Atwater-Kent car-battery-powered radio in the twenties just seemed to send him daydreaming, sitting on the white fluffy clouds of summer skies. These beautiful sounds of music from Fred Waring and the Pennsylvanians, Sammy Kay, Guy Lombardo, along with the songs of Jerome Kern and the Gershwins, who possessed the golden pens of music, coupled with the movie stars of the silver screen, put within the heart of this now-teenage boy a love that would never die. These beautiful experiences caused me to begin the search for the beau-

2

tiful lady (the angel from heaven) that I believed God would send me one day.

Even Isaiah marveled at the strength of a love song: "I will sing for the One I love a song about His vineyard. My loved One had a vineyard on a fertile hillside" (Is. 5:1).

My mother, Susie Alice, always saw to it that her four daughters and three sons went to Sunday school. I was in Mrs. Steele's "overall" class. She was such a nice lady, even if her son-in-law was a millionaire who promoted the large lead and zinc mining fields of Oronogo. Mrs. Steele knew the plight of the poor people of our town. She had all of us boys wear overalls to her class so we all seemed the same, even her grandson, with all his father's money.

She always made sure we memorized one Bible verse every week. I guess I was about seven or eight years old then. After Sunday school, I always loved to sit by my mother in church because she had such a beautiful alto voice. I always had to sing loud to stay in tune and harmonize with her. When I did well, Mom would always look at me and just smile her approval. I guess that was the beginning of my love for music and my lasting affiliation with God. God and music made life happy, and my mother seemed to know that.

My mother would say to me, while I was camped by the old radio and listening to the song "Deep Purple" or "The Way You Look Tonight," performed by Fred Waring, "C.E., you are going to turn into music."

At this age, I was trusted to walk downtown, about twelve to fifteen blocks, to Mr. Board's Drug Store to play pool and snack on a Mr. Goodbar and a Coke, a treat from Mom and Dad.

I marveled at the older neighbors, sitting on their porches just swinging away. As I walked by, they would take time to visit with me. The wisdom and advice they all gave made me wise for my age; at least I was told that many times. What a blessing it would be if every boy in the world could be as blessed and as happy as I was.

3

Poor? No, I was rich. So very rich.

Years have just flown by, and here I'm seventy years old, but these boyhood joys only seem a few days ago. All my very sweet friends say, "C.E., one would think you many years younger." I am always thankful and reply, "Happiness will do that, don'tcha know."

When winter came, twenty-five or thirty boys and girls would congregate at the old Circle Pond, when it was frozen over, to ice-skate. We would build a large campfire and skate until 9:00 P.M. almost every night, as long as the ice was safe. This pond was about eight to ten acres, and when summertime came it was our fishing hole. It was surely the fun place in this little old mining town, which boasted of being one of the largest open-pit mining operations in the country for lead, zinc, and ore.

The "Roaring Twenties" had just ended and the depression years of the thirties were in full swing; it seemed everyone was so very poor. Government handouts in those days were unheard of. People just stuck together, friend helping friend, cultivating trust and love in communities and towns across America. We were a happy and loving people in spite of the hard times.

How can anything so precious to life be trodden under the dust of time and forgotten by people who call themselves Americans—America, a nation God has truly showered with blessings?

Reflecting back, shouldn't we all be ashamed of ourselves for trading these attributes for the worldly corruption of today?

Two things I never told my mother before she died are as follows:

In my group of friends—Alley Rats, as we were called—I was the daredevil. The very large open-pit mining cave, when full of water, was about three hundred feet deep from the surface. The water was as blue as the ocean. It was thought of as one of the largest open-pit lead and zinc mining operations in the country. The walls in this pit were almost vertical, with the exception of large rock jetties. One such jetty was between twenty-five and thirty-five feet

4

above the cold blue water. Being the athletic kid on the block, I was always dared to do crazy things first. All these Alley Rats thought if I didn't make it jackknifing or swan diving off that rock jetty, then they wouldn't have to do it. As usual, I survived. When it came their turn, at times we almost had to give some a little help.

The second thing I never told my mother was about Mr. Buener, the grandfather of a boy named Max, who was one of the Alley Rats. Mr. Buener had a cellar, and on hot summer days we would sit on the bottom step after playing a hard game of baseball, because it was so cool there. One day the padlock was not locked, so Ma opened the door. Inside was a large wooden barrel with a spigot and a tin cup nearby. *Boy,* we thought. *Grape juice is sure cool and sweet.* Well, it didn't take long for about five or six fifteen-year-olds to be put away. When he managed to awaken us all did we catch it. That old German gent sure could cuss. That was my first encounter with the "spirits". . . . Mother, please forgive me.

With the eleventh year of high school completed, my education was finished in the Oronogo school system. It did not offer a twelfth grade.

I opted to go to the Carl Junction High School, which furnished a school bus to our town. The year was 1937 and the power of God was steering me to this school instead of Webb City High School. The very first day of the fall term, the angel I thought God would send me just passed before my eyes. It was so evident, because my heart pounded like it would burst. So beautiful was she—starry green eyes, raven black hair, bobby socks, and penny loafer shoes. This really special feeling was destined to live in the hearts of this young couple for a lifetime of a true kind of love.

This beautiful girl, Ellie, and I had study hall in the same afternoon period. The first time I asked her for a date the request was in the form of a note passed to her by one of her girlfriends, who sat behind me in study hall. Ellie's reply was: "I'm going roller skating; maybe we could meet there."

Boy! That was almost a yes! Meet we did, at the West Seventh

Street rink, which was just a large circus-type tent with a wooden floor. It wasn't a fancy place like rinks are today, with snack bars, etc.

We had such a good time getting to know something about each other. Ellie was really a good skater. She was very athletic yet so graceful that every move seemed effortless and precise. Before we knew it, 10:00 P.M. was there. Ellie's two older sisters had brought her to the skating rink, and not knowing me at all, would not let me take her home. We didn't even get a little friendly peck. But just standing there and holding hands with this very pretty girl was a thrill for me.

Years later, we all four laughed about this many, many times. Her sisters would always say, "C.E., we knew you were a bad dude."

I was invited to Ellie's mother and stepfather's home the next week and I guess I was approved, because the next night was Friday and I got to take Ellie to the movies. At fifteen years old, Ellie seemed so mature, like me at the age of seventeen. That was the beginning of our love for the musical movies. However, we were unaware of the young puppy-love obstacles ahead.

A beautiful, popular girl with a not-so-bad boy caused some problems trying to get through our teens. I guess you could call it young jealousy. Being head cheerleader and Drum Corps majorette, this beautiful girl was an attention getter, and this C.E., the out-of-town Oronogo boy, was the school's best track performer and the baseball pitcher to win the most games at CJHS.

The thrill of the dating was destined for romance.

Christmas marked our first year of puppy love. Ellie gave me such a beautiful blue and gray knit tie, and every Christmas after was not the same if she didn't get me a beautiful tie. Christmas Day was a white Christmas, and I drove to Mrs. Moon's house, ten miles away, in my dad's car to give Ellie her gift. The gate to the driveway was locked, so I jumped over the fence, falling in the snow but holding Ellie's gift above my head so it didn't break. Ellie's mother answered the door and asked me in. She was making breakfast on the old wood stove: bacon, eggs, biscuits, fried potatoes, and gravy. I hadn't had breakfast yet so, boy, this delicious smell was getting to me.

Mrs. Moon offered me a place at the table while she went to awaken Ellie, who had not appeared as yet. This country breakfast was just out of sight. Finally, Ellie appeared, wiping the sleep from her eyes and fluffing her beautiful black hair. When she saw me at the table with this pretty package, she almost yelled, "Is this for me?"

Her beautiful green eyes were just sparkling with joy. When she opened this Evening In Paris makeup set with a brush and comb, fingernail stuff, face powder, and perfume, she hugged me so tight, in her mother's presence—which was a no-no in 1937. I can still feel the magic and the joy of that Christmas morning.

Little did I know that Ellie's mother would be like a second mother to me, as well as one of my very best friends. Later on, I loved to hear her call me C.C., not C.E.

Mrs. Moon let Ellie go to the movies twice a week, but she always had to be home on time. We just loved Nelson Eddy and Jeanette MacDonald movies. Their singing was so beautiful. It seemed that the sweet love stories of the movies taught Ellie and me to be sweethearts with trusting love, one for the other.

Respecting one another for what our mothers taught us, we were virgins to one another all through our young dating life. I'm sure this pleased God, for He filled our whole lifetime together with the rarest of true love.

Our long-time minister's wife said of us, "You are truly a beautiful, special couple. I cannot see one of you without the other . . . ever."

My boyhood school friend Rex and I were schoolmates from the first grade in Oronogo until our senior year in CJHS. We double-dated most of the time, because cars were hard to come by. Rex was the baby of his family. His brother and sister were married, so his parents made sure Rex had dating money. Sometimes he would have as much as ten dollars, while most guys like me were lucky to have fifty cents.

Rex's father would let us use his car a couple of nights a week, but I had to drive. Mr. Keys would get me off to the side and give me a couple of dollars for gasoline but would always tell me not to let Rex drive. He just trusted me, and even as young as I was, I honored that.

I would borrow my uncle's car several times a month, so that kept me and Ellie's dating just great. One night after the movies, we went to the C & A Drive-In for Cokes before going home. I asked Ellie if she wanted a hamburger, which was a mistake, because she said, "Yes . . . and a Coke." Well, the movie cost twenty cents for the both of us, the Cokes were another twenty, and the hamburger was a dime. That was exactly the amount of money I had. Was that luck or what?

I knew I could depend on Rex for a loan, but that would be embarrassing in front of my girl. Over the years, we have enjoyed many good times laughing about that night that you may call "big-time" dating in the 1930s.

The spring of 1938 was here and it was graduation time for me.

New clothes were hard to come by in those days, but I had seen a white sports jacket in the window at Coulter McGuire's Men's Store in Joplin. I wanted it so much. My mother knew that and let me add the five dollars it cost to the family grocery bill at Woodward's Grocery Store. Boy, I thought I was somebody in that white sports coat. I paid the five dollars back to our grocery account out of my first check from my first job after graduation.

Do you think that one could borrow money for such a cause from the town grocery today? I doubt it, too. These hard times were filled with beautiful people.

I was honored to be chosen to sing the graduation solo. My mother was so proud, she thanked Mr. Rice, the music director. He made her so happy when he confirmed that I was one of his best senior students. Ellie complimented me also by saying, "You sang your song good." That sounds so funny to me now, I just chuckle.

Dating after graduation, we heard the beautiful song "All The Things You Are," by Jerome Kern. This love song was destined to foster a lifetime of love between Ellie and me. I hope the reader knows the words of this song because they are glowing, breathless words heaven sent for two young people so in love. The words describe exactly as pictured in my mind this beautiful girl of fifteen whom I know God would send me one day. She was my angel and God has watched over us ever since.

During Ellie's junior year, CJHS formed its first drum corps and many applicants auditioned for Drum Corps majorette. But there was no doubt in my mind that my girl would get this coveted honor. She was the most beautiful girl, the most talented marching girl, and the most athletic girl not only in our school, but in the whole school district. Mr. Rice, our music director, chose correctly when he chose Ellie. Boy, did Ellie and I have fun celebrating that victory.

Just to prove a point on Mr. Rice's choice, he entered our Drum Corps in the Joplin (Missouri) Fiesta Celebration Parade, which was a big event for the Four-State Area (Kansas, Oklahoma, Arkansas, and Missouri). Thousands of people thronged into Joplin. When the parade got under way, we could hardly wait until our Drum Corps marched by the judges' stand. I stood almost all afternoon with my fingers crossed. These young ladies, with only two years' experience, marched away with first place honors. Ellie's mother, Mrs. Moon, and I were so happy, I could just see it in Ellie's eyes.

This is not the last time you will hear of this most memorable day. I still get chill bumps just thinking about it, even if it was over fifty years ago.

Ellie's junior-senior play was called *Hawaii.* Boy, she was dynamite. We went to the kids' hangout, C & A Drive-In, for ten-cent hamburgers and ten-cent Cokes after the play. That night,

Ellie: first Drum Corps majorette, CJHS, 1938 first-place winner.

we made our long-distance plans to go to Hawaii on our twenty-fifth wedding anniversary. Such big talk from little kids. I just can't help but believe God must have inspired Jerome Kern to write the aformentioned song, "All The Things You Are," for Ellie and me.

My father died in 1939, leaving my mother with my seven brothers and sisters and no means of support. Before that, he was sick for a long time, so off I had gone to work in the lead and zinc mines to support the family. Most of the lead and zinc mining shafts were around three hundred feet deep, and workers rode down in an open ore bucket, approximately five feet by five feet, at about thirty-five miles an hour. It was scary to begin with and I just held on for life until the hoister man sat it gently on the bottom platform.

When the workers finally got out of this metal bucket, we picked up our picks and shovels and walked up to the heading, which was a wall the night crew had blasted with dynamite, so we could shovel these large buckets full of the ore dirt.

I was just a teenager, weighing about 159 pounds, while all the rest of the shovelers were grown men, around 200 pounds. They liked me because I was just a determined, tough kid. When I would shovel up to a large rock, two or three guys would say, "Watch out, kid, this one will almost fill your bucket." That's how we got paid, by the bucket. Three or four dollars a day was really good for a hard rock miner in 1939.

My mother, Susie Alice, hated to see her oldest son work in the place that had caused his father to get sick. But it put food on the table and clothes on all of us, and I had a few dollars left so I could see my Ellie on regular dates.

However, you see, here came God to my rescue. The boss got me a job in the ore mill before I got addicted to working underground, where it was so cool, which all miners will tell you is like smoking cigarettes.

The ore mill was only about a mile from the mines. I worked the graveyard shift, so when Ellie and I had a date I really had to put on the steam to get to work at midnight.

The summers were so lonely, because Ellie would go on vacation with her sister Chloe to California and the Colorado mountains where her brother Bill lived. I just loved to hear about her trips because twenty miles from Joplin was the extent of my travel.

On our first date after Ellie got home from vacation in the summer of 1939, I surprised her by giving her an engagement ring which she accepted with those beautiful green eyes full of happy tears and a sweet smile that just melted my heart away.

I had purchased the set of rings while Ellie was on vacation. It was the first credit purchase I ever made. Dratchenburg Jewelry, in Webb City, let me pay them off at something less than five dollars a month. My mother encouraged me to pay them off early, which I did. What a blessing that I did, because hard times struck again. The lead and zinc mines and mill shut down and left me unemployed. This slowed down our dating even though gasoline was only eight cents a gallon. Fortunately, my first car, a 1934 Ford coupe with a rumble seat and red wire wheels, was also paid off early.

I was so desperate to find other work that I took a job offer from a town friend we'll call Jody to work in a Santa Fe Railroad repair gang in Denver, Colorado. However, this was put off for a week or so because this was the time when my father was very ill. He was a tough man and an ex-boxer. He didn't go to church with Mother and the family. He was a blue-flint hard-rock mining boss. He managed the Oronogo Blues baseball team also.

The underground mining job had given him silicosis, and when he was bedridden and so very sick, he took my hand and said, "C.E., you are my oldest son. Will you please take care of your mother and brothers and sisters?" I promised I would. Little did I know, at this time, that this promise might cause me to lose my girl, Ellie.

Dad's sister was a preacher of the Nazarene faith, and he asked me to have her come and pray for him. She did, and so did our family. I trust God heard all of us and forgave Dad's sins and opened the Pearly Gates of Heaven.

Now it was time for my friend Jody and me to hop a freight train and bum our way to Colorado and extra gang work. We hit the rails, and a few days later we arrived in Denver at night and were side-railed at Littleton, just south of Denver. Jody and I disembarked that night and, while walking the railroad tracks, found a culvert with some large pasteboard boxes, which we used for sleeping and to keep warm during the cold night.

We looked around the next morning and saw a nice truck garden. We climbed the fence and picked a melon for breakfast. A little man started yelling at us, and our first impulse was to run out of there. But Jody said, "He wants us to come see him." Which we did.

We learned his name was Kay Shomoto, and he was a Japanese gardener. He gave us a job and fixed us a place to stay: room and board, so to speak. Kay and Mrs. Shomoto and their son and daughter were kind to us for about a month before we went to work for the railroad. Little did I know, then, I would be asked to fight against their countrymen in the upcoming World War II.

This was so hard to understand at such a young age. I guess in a way, as rough and tough as I was, I was also a little tender-hearted, because I could still see my mama standing on the front porch in Oronogo, wiping her tears with her apron as I was leaving for Colorado. My two youngest sisters, Melba, age four, and Jeanie, age six, followed after me through the gate. I stooped to pick Melba up and took Jeanie by the hand back through the gate and assured them I'd be back soon.

Soon after, Jody and I were hired for the Santa Fe railroad gang. We were sleeping in wall bunkbeds, eating in the central diner boxcars, and working on blazing hot railroad tracks with jackhammer-type tools. Tie tamping was tough work. However, I could send almost all my pay to my mothers, brothers, and sisters.

Ellie, her sister Chloe, and Chloe's husband, E.J., came to see me on their vacation while I was working on the railroads. They were going to Idaho Springs, Colorado, forty miles west of Denver, to the mountains where Ellie's brother Bill lived. Idaho Springs was a little gold mining town and tough, like my hometown of Oronogo.

Brother Bill and his wife, Helen, went back to Denver with us to a matinee dance place and we danced the afternoon away. On the way back up the mountains, we stopped so Bill could take our picture along the roadside. As we got out of the car, a round watermelon rolled out with us, so Ellie and I picked it up as they shot our photo. That picture is on our bedroom wall fifty-four years later.

The railroad work all summer had moved our repair crew from Littleton to the Kansas state line, and I told my friend Jody I was going to quit and return to Pueblo, Colorado, about one hundred miles back up the road, so Ellie and I could be married and live there.

The light air and beautiful mountains had helped to ease my lonely time without her. We had written each other every week and it seemed like we asked so many questions, but "I love you" was in almost every line.

I hitched a ride back to Pueblo and for five dollars a month got a room at 925 Court Street, which was owned by a dentist and his wife. Their office was in the front room and they lived in the rear area of the first floor and rented out rooms upstairs. After paying my rent and sending money to my mother, I had enough left for about a week of meals. I had forgotten the depression was still on, and the days of job searching soon exhausted my nest-egg money. I never drank so much water in my life.

Three days of this diet were enough for this guy. On awakening the third day of no food, I dressed at 5:30 A.M. and walked to the little café on Union Street where I had eaten several times. I ordered breakfast and, as I finished, the owner gave me the ticket and I told him I was broke and couldn't pay, but I would work all day for the meal. He was angry but finally agreed. I never saw so many pots.

Ellie's little tan coat (1940). Young love! Never got old.

The next day, as I was job-hunting on Union Street at six in the morning, I saw a little fat man sweeping the sidewalk in front of his bakery. I asked him to let me sweep it for breakfast. He said, "Get out of here! You're not a bum; you have a suit and tie on."

I assured him I was hungry. He stopped sweeping, leaned on the broom, and looked at me. He then walked to the doorway of his bakery, leaned the broom against the window, and took me next door to John's Café, where we had breakfast together.

For this nineteen-year-old boy it was a blessing, for days to come. A beautiful friendship was being born. This sweet gentleman's name was Steve Monach, and he let me work moving 100-pound sacks of flour and sweeping out the entire bakery. Can't you see me doing this with a nice dark green suit on? I was soon white as a summer cloud, but I didn't care; I was on track and doing what I wanted, and working. Before the day's end, God came into this bakery, because the bakery's city deliveryman, named Pat, came in and told Mr. Monach that he was leaving that day to go to Texas. Mr. Monach looked over to me and smiled. I think, now, that God must have whispered in his ear from the look on his face as he asked if I wanted the job. Fifteen dollars a week. Boy, did I!

Mr. and Mrs. Monach were Czechoslovakians, from the old country. They had four lovely daughters and no son. As time went by, they seemed to treat me as a son. Mary (Mrs. Monach) would bring lunch and sometimes dinner to the bakery, and the Monachs always invited me to eat with them. Gee! It was so very good, and their sharing their love with me was so super. Steve (Mr. Monach) first urged me to write this book in the year 1940. Well, my good friend, it's taken fifty-four years to comply with your wishes. God almighty knows I love you for it.

A few years passed by and Steve and Mary were blessed with their own son, Stephen Jr. He was so loved by his sisters, Rose Mary, Pat, Barbara, and Rita. What a lovely family. Steve Jr. now owns the bakery, as Steve and Mary have gone to heaven.

In June of 1940, Ellie came to Pueblo by bus and we hoped to be married. When Ellie came, it seemed God had just opened the doors of heaven. We were so happy to be with each other, if only for a week. However, I was still helping my mother and family meet their bills. Ellie and I discussed the finance problem and agreed, with remorse, that maybe we should postpone our plans. It just about killed us for her to leave for Carl Junction.

My father had taught me that a man is no better than his word, so the bedside promise I made to my dying father might very well ruin my life with the only girl I ever loved. But, you see, I was so young that I overlooked the power of God, and He wasn't going to let that happen.

Even though we were engaged, Ellie and I agreed to have other friends, but no serious ones. Well, you know, when a beautiful girl is free to date she has all kinds of offers. A couple of boys wanted her to give me back the engagement ring.

Also, I had several dancing dates with a pretty Spanish lady. It wasn't serious for me, but she was, so that put an end to our dancing together. I don't hesitate to say she was a sweet pretty lady and we did enjoy dancing together many times.

From the Banquet Bakery I would deliver pies, cakes, and doughnuts to a neighborhood grocery store, Ray's Grocery and Meat Market, on East Eighth Street. I noticed they were asking me a lot of questions; however, I was so young I didn't give it much thought. They later asked me to come and work for them, operating their large delivery route all over the city of Pueblo. This store was owned by two brothers, Joe and Fred, and the butcher Ray. They all were nice to me and we became good friends even though they were older than Ellie and me. When I went to work for them I was given a three-dollar-a-week raise in pay.

It wasn't too long before my mother got a job at the Oronogo Post Office. This relieved my part of the support. I had also taken the better-paying job at Ray's. Now, can you see how perfectly God's plan was working?

A few months went by and, as I was sweeping the storefront

steps, I saw Ellie getting out of her sister's car. I dropped that broom and we ran to each other with outstretched arms and embraced on the streetcar tracks in the middle of the street. We didn't know if a streetcar was coming and really didn't care. With teary eyes, cheek to cheek, we just knew God had truly given us to each other today.

Just a few days later, we were married in the Reverend Rowland Hill's house across the street from where I worked.

Now, do you recall the song "All The Things You Are"? Well the last verse tells the story of how Ellie and I now are one, as God ordained that all we are now belongs to each other and we are in the powerful hands of God. From our first meeting in 1937, to the day the angels came for Ellie (57 years), He nurtured this most unusual love every day of our lives.

When I left Missouri, I also left my first car for my mother. A boy's first car is something very special in his life, but for family one must not be selfish. It only upset me to know my younger brothers tore up this lovely car. That was never mentioned again to me in my life.

To get married without a car was no problem for me and my girl after all we had gone though for the love and blessings that were ours. We were so in love that nothing mattered except each of us being together forever. When we had paid all of our bills every week, we had only enough money to buy each other an ice-cream cone at the White Rock Café on Main Street.

"The True Measure" is a lovely saying by any standard. Ellie and I often said to each other we didn't know anyone who was in love and romantic every day as we were—it was our way of life. It fueled our happiness. It kept us so very young; spiritually, mentally, and physically. Love enabled us to live life vigorously, yet serenely. Love never needed a wakeup call for Ellie and me. That was "The True Measure," don'tcha see?

As I stare at it now, the happy tears are so hard to hold. I wonder if the author Johann Goethe knew this would happen when it caught up with the couple it was written about. How sweet and beautiful

heart to survive whatever came my way. This made me a top marine combat medic, pharmacist mate, first-class petty officer of the First Marine Division, Fifth Regiment, Company B, First Medical Battalion.

The days, months, and years ahead were unbelievable. The destruction and pain and death are almost untold in its entirety. As previously recorded, "War is hell." Mr. Churchill said it right from his easy chair, but we experienced it firsthand on deadly beaches and in foxholes and tank traps where so many were detained forever. God have mercy.

It was in such a place the First Marines encountered fierce opposition on Peleliu Island. We had survived Zero attacks and banzai attacks in a tank trap on this day. Just off the airport runway, we were recipients of blistering machine-gun and mortar attacks. The noise was so devastating it even made our noses bleed.

Mortar shells fell into our tank trap fragments, piercing the flesh. I saw our company commander, (Dr.) Capt. Ralph Budge, was hit bad: a six-inch-by-half-inch piece of mortar shell had lodged in his neck just below his helmet. He was bleeding very badly. After pain shots and a compress to curb the bleeding, no one wanted to run him on a litter across the open airport runway to a first-aid station so he could be sent to the hospital ships waiting offshore. This was the only chance Dr. Budge had to survive.

A medic from Arkansas named Tucker was holding the litter. I said, "Tucker, let's go." And go we did.

We managed to escape all enemy firing and ran like hell for the beach evacuation station, which was about half a mile from our tank trap. As we jostled Dr. Budge on the litter, we could see bullets kicking up the coral and sand on the airport runway with another hundred yards yet to go. Now, can't you see how God was watching over us?

Tucker said later, "Pittman, you almost ran away from the captain and me."

I could run fast because I had learned from high school track.

23

Those zinging bullets helped to speed us up also. I bet Dr. Budge had bruises from the bouncing later, but what counted was that we were successful in our interacting.

Poor old Tucker was a smoker, and it took the longest time for him to get his breath back. As for me, I didn't smoke, so no problem. I was in good physical condition and that's why I was always selected to go on reconnaissance patrol to scout out enemy locations as a combat medic with marine scouting troops.

How very fast you could learn from the local birds and mammals where the enemy was. It was an eerie feeling to be out in the jungle with such a small party of marines. We were so lucky, I only know of one casualty on all these missions in which I participated.

When we set the litter down easily, after such a rough ride, Captain Budge looked up at us and said, "You men should get the Silver Star for this. And, Pittman, if that blood on you is what I think it is, a Purple Heart also."

We never saw or heard of Captain Budge again, and none of the foregoing came true. However, I think that brave guy Tucker believed, as I did, that accommodations and medals were no trade-off for life. Our ultimate blessing from heaven was our life. We were still alive, dog-tired, dirty, thirsty, hungry, and sleepy, but still on our feet. Thank you, Sweet Jesus.

The First Marine Division was known as the "old breed" of fighting men. We, the front-line combat medics, called ourselves the "special breed." We not only did our best to save a fellow marine's life, but at times we stood toe to toe, firing away at the enemy positions.

I noticed the *VFW Magazine* quoted from Henry Berry's book and Major Frank Hough's book in their article about the Peleliu Island invasion. Why they refused this author, who participated with the first marine landing on Peleliu Island, is a mystery. However, the landing was difficult because coral reefs fanned so far out to sea that it made ship landing impossible, so we came ashore by landing barges until the sea was so shallow that we ran aground fifty or one hundred yards offshore. This left us like sitting ducks, trying to wade ashore up to our chest on the surf. The toll of dead bobbed in the sea all around us. This sight told us we were in deep trouble as mortar shells exploded all around us in the water. We who survived didn't get off the beach until the following day.

The temperature on Peleliu was scorching hot, some days 115° Fahrenheit or more. The Japanese crushed white coral for airport runways and when the sun was at midday (12:00 noon) the glare and heat was unbelievable. The U.S. bombers and war ships had stripped the island of all trees by repeated bombing and shelling, so shade from the sun was eliminated.

I'm told this conflict required between 500 and 1000 ships, thousands of aircraft and thousand after thousands of fighting men, some of which lay lifeless in the surf and the airport runways and tank traps which were all over the island.

After securing Peleliu, our First Marine Division was to be shipped to a rest area for regrouping and planning the Okinawa beachhead a short time later.

The day that we were scheduled to leave Peleliu, a storm out at sea caused a very high surf (maybe twenty-five-foot swells). It was difficult to even board the small landing craft that took us to the waiting transport ship. It was almost impossible. Those of us who were lucky enough to make the mile or two to the waiting ships had to climb rope ladders (nets) approximately fifty to sixty feet to the ship's top deck. Please remember, we were carrying fifty- to seventy-five-pound backpacks and firearms. It was not very easy!

Several climbers lost their foothold and fell back down into our small landing craft. If one was directly below them, you would be pinned to the boat's bottom. Now that hurts, I can tell you for sure. Once on deck safely, I glanced back at the island which once was just hell, but now so peaceful. Why—why is man so desperate for power? Memories are left so ugly in one's mind.

Even those of us whom God blessed with survival can't

obliterate this day after day of hell and devastation from island to island, beachhead to beachhead, even after fifty years.

You would think one tour would be all the combat one would be asked to do, especially if one was a family man with children, but not so. After Peleliu, we who had high points of combat duty and a lot of replacements were granted thirty days' family leave in February 1945. You just can't imagine what happy moments Ellie, Patricia, and I had after being so far away from each other for so long (about twenty months of just plain hell).

Our little family of three sure tried to make up for the long separation in just thirty days. As our time vanished and I had to report back, I said, "Ellie, as soon as I know where they will station me, I'll write you a letter and you and Pat come meet me there."

I had no idea they would send us back into combat a second time in one war. How wrong I was. Oh, how I hated to write that letter to Ellie. I just knew it would break her heart, as it did mine. I almost got the brig for mouthing off at the officer that gave us our second overseas duty orders. Damn, I sure was mad!

My friend Whitie just kept pushing me down the line, saying, "Shut your damned mouth, Pittman."

As soon as Company B, First Medical Battalion, Fifth Regiment, First Marines reported in at the California base, I and several others were assigned to join the First Marines in the Philippines to be deployed to beachheads at Okinawa. How is that for the law of averages, to try to survive again? Just the expectation of more of what we had gone through was almost as difficult on one's mind as the actual beachhead landings themselves.

The tragedy of all this was that those who were asked to live in this hell were also supposed to carry a pad and pen to make notes of all injuries and illnesses so they could be registered on records. No accommodations were ever given for sleepless nights, two or three in a row, in a foxhole knee-deep in mud and water, wearing bloodstained dungarees. We brushed our teeth with salt tablets and our fingers; we took baths without soap when it rained and put our dirty clothing back on what we called a clean body.

Of course, this was thrown in extra, along with the Japanese Zeros' diving runs, banzai attacks, screaming enemy machine-gun fire, and mortar attacks. Don't you agree this atmosphere was just made for bookwork or pad-and-pencil stuff?

Well, this seems to have been the thinking of those who drew up the phrase *service-connected disability.* When one is questioned by a Veterans Affair officer who asks, "Have you ever been shot at or subjected to severe enemy mortar or machine-gun fire?" and our answer is "Yes," the first thing they want to do is put you in a group undergoing mental therapy.

I love America—it is my home—and I would do the foregoing all over again. However, it is impossible to sanction the thoughts and actions of the U.S. officials who don't know or don't care about the most deserving veterans, the ones who put their life on the line not once or twice, but for month after month. I can see these rules applying to stateside noncombatants who had the luxury of liberty every night; dancing, cocktails, and steak dinners; clean beds, clean clothes, and showers. But when an infantry combat veteran asks for medication to relieve his body of a dangerous condition and is told: "It's not service-connected and the guidelines do not furnish this expensive medicine [sixty dollars a month] unless it is service-connected," you can see that after Uncle Sam says: "I want you!" and promises almost anything, the beat of the drums now can hardly be heard when it comes to honoring the battlescarred private, seaman, "dog-face," GI Joe, or marine who was the backbone of America's victory in World War II.

God forgive you all for thinking we weren't even worth sixty dollars a month.

As we were being prepared to be shipped from the Philippines to Okinawa, the Japanese surrendered and World War II was history. Lord have mercy on us all for doing what we had to do.

Shipping was standing by to take the first wave of marines

with the most combat points to the good old USA. I was in the midst of this group, and we sailed home on our ship with very little crew and food aboard. We were to disembark at Portland, Oregon. Because of the short crew, I was master-at-arms of a crew of six on deck watch from midnight to 4:00 A.M. The old boat lost one of its screws (propellers) on the way and slowed our arrival. It took us thirty-three days to reach the mouth of the Columbia River on the Oregon coast. This was disastrous, because food was in short supply. It was hardtack, grapefruit, and fish soup almost every day. Some days we got beans for breakfast, lunch, and dinner.

As we made our way up the Columbia River, the fish-canning factory docks were lined with welcoming workers; hundreds and hundreds of people gave us a homecoming welcome.

After disembarking, we got immediate leave to get a real steak dinner in Portland. Not knowing the war was ending, I had sent Ellie my last paycheck, so I was broke. The guys would not let me stay and eat ship's food. A really nice marine from New Hampshire loaned me dinner money. I never paid him back, as I lost the paper with his name and address. So every Christmas I put folding money in a bell ringer's pot and say a blessing for this marine. I hope, in some way, he knows this. I was so grateful for his kindness.

Our troop train arrived and we were so anxious to board. The train was chugging along on its way to Joplin and my precious waiting family, who didn't even know I was on my way. I thought, prayerfully, *It seems God is always giving Ellie back to me, especially at the times that seem so hopeless.* To profess His Name among men now would be truly a blessing for Ellie and me. As we have often said: "He has always lighted the lamp in our lives so we would never lose the way."

As I knocked on the door of Ellie and Pat's house, I saw my beautiful lady open the door. I thought she would faint. I cannot express the feeling that went through us at this moment; Webster didn't include the word in his book to describe this precious time.

As I look back at this reunion, I think God must have had to rest also after three years of watching over us, which was no easy task.

By the picture of Christ is a plaque that I had given Ellie which shows a little girl telling a little boy that he's somebody because she loves him. As they are holding each other in a fond embrace she puts her hand on his heart, as Ellie had done once on a mountaintop years before.

Ellie and C.E. "High Country!" Mount Evans, Colorado.
"The Real Westerners," 1970.

3

The hit song "Once in Every Life" tells us that it's not very often that someone so sweet and beautiful comes along in our life, as my Ellie did to me. She was just the "true measure." My lady, my love, my life, Ellie was my girl.

Our hearts and minds were so anxious to return to Colorado, which we did after a short visit with my family. We pulled into Pueblo, rented an apartment, and drove up to Idaho Springs, west of Denver, to visit Ellie's brother and his wife. They insisted we stay a week or so, which was great fun.

A deep snow fell during the night before the day we planned to return to Pueblo. We were warned it was too dangerous to go down the mountain to Denver. In spite of the objections of Ellie's brother and his wife, Helen, we left. It was just a short time before we saw cars overturned and off the mountainside, so I stopped and put Ellie and Patricia on the backseat floor and wrapped them in a blanket for their safety. God just sat there beside me as I put our car in low gear and proceeded down the forty miles to Denver and on south to our apartment.

The following days found Ellie making Pat and me a lovely place to live and I was there at Kress & Company, picking up where I had left off about three years earlier. Time just rushed by as every day was so new and exciting.

As the birth of our second child came on January 31, 1947, the thrill of God's visit to our home was the same as when our beautiful daughter was given to us. We named the baby boy Donald Eugene. He was a beautiful, healthy boy except for infant colic, which kept us awake many nights. I would lay him across my

31

stomach and pat his bottom to get him to sleep. As he began to grow healthy, we four loved to picnic in City Park after swimming.

Our old car was about played out and our dear friends at Ray's Grocery and Meat Market helped us get a 1946 Plymouth, which was very hard to get this soon after the war. Ray's family owned the auto agency, and that was a blessing from old friends.

Having this new car enabled us to go to Missouri on vacation to see Ellie's mother, now called Grandma Lilly by our children. It allowed me to visit my family as well.

At the Kress store, I was good at what I did. The district manager and the New York office gave me my first store in Arkansas City, Kansas. I left early to find us a nice place to live. Ellie and the children were driven down by Mrs. Edwards, a sweet neighbor lady. Life in this small Kansas town was slow and easy, which gave us time to really enjoy our family.

The store closed at 9:00 on Saturday nights, and sometimes we all packed into the car to drive to Carl Junction to see Grandma Lilly and George Moon, Ellie's stepfather. It was such a happy time, if only for a few hours, as Sunday afternoon found us going west on old Kansas Highway 166 to Arkansas City.

Before leaving Grandma Lilly, between hugs and tears, I would slip a few dollars in Lilly's hand and whisper, "Buy yourself something nice." Through her tears she would look up at me and say, "OK, C.C." Isn't that nice? (She always called me C.C. for some reason.)

I was a good merchandiser and store manager, and with the cooperation of my employees our Kansas store achieved nice profits for Kress & Company in my two-year tenure. My reward was the promotion to a much larger store, maybe ten times larger. This, on the surface, was almost unbelievable. However, my new district manager and I were not so compatible and some friction occurred. Jefferson City, Missouri, was my next store to conquer.

Ellie's little prayer book expressed our gratitude for our almost perfect life together perfectly: "O Lord, in my 'success,' help me never to forget that what I am is more important than what I do. Remind me again and again that faith stimulates success, but only love sanctifies success. I can not and dare not succeed without Your Love and Power in my life." As Ellie always said: "Thank you, Sweet Jesus. Amen."

As our life in Jefferson City moved slowly along, we were having a difficult time finding a nice home for our family in the crowded capital city. Our sweet old friends in Pueblo, Mr. and Mrs. Steve Monach, had written us a nice letter congratulating us on our promotion, and I'm sure Ellie was missing good friends like them. In our return letter to the Monachs, Ellie mentioned the housing problem and, would you know, a few days later there came another letter from Steve and Mary. As Ellie opened the envelope, she could see the check inside. We almost fainted at the four-digit figure. Boy, that was a lot of money in 1949–50. It was a loan from two sweet, godly people to supply our need. There were no IOU papers to sign, just a short letter saying: "Just pay when you can, no interest and no time limit."

I'm baffled yet today at this magnitude of God's love for earthlings like us. However, the precious gift was never used for its intended purpose.

My district manager and I were still having problems. As I was signing the store payroll, I noticed the cashier's salary was more than my monthly pay as manager. I confronted my supervisor, asking him if I was being deprived of the higher pay because of my three years' absence during the war. His reply, as I remember, was something like this: "It's not the company's fault that the war came." Immediately I asked to be replaced and advised him a letter of resignation would go forward, this date, to Mr. Baker, Personnel Vice President, as was required by the central office. Ellie and I discussed this at length, and she concurred.

We wrote a very, very thankful letter to the Monachs including the check, voided and uncashed. In our hearts was a thankful "Amen," as always.

We went back to Carl Junction to Grandma Lilly's. The very first day we found a nice place to live and put Patricia back in school. Little did we know our love for each other was just beginning to unfold in such a special way.

To keep the money flow up, I got a job selling new cars for a company at B and Main Street in Joplin. The Carl Junction School Board filing date for our locality was at hand, so I filed and won. I served two terms while our children were in school there.

Sperry Vickers, Inc., in Joplin, had an opening in the purchasing department for which I applied, but I heard no answer. After a school board meeting, I drove by the plant manager's home one evening. After apologizing for the late intrusion, I asked for an interview the following morning and got the job as purchasing agent for MRO Products. This very good job helped Ellie and me to purchase our first new home, at 2827 Joplin Street, Joplin, Missouri.

After all our problems a few months previously, Ellie was so thrilled. She always made sure I knew that, in her own special way. Oh, how I loved to give her the best things life would afford us. When I related that to her, she would look deeply into my eyes and say, "C.E., you are the best thing in life to me." It made me feel like Samson or Atlas, just super! Love is like that, you know.

We were very successful with planning all of Vickers's parties, picnics, and dances and were commended many times by the corporate office. Vickers's employment was 1,500, so our activities required a large facility, and Memorial Hall benefited us properly. I just loved to show off Ellie, who always was so beautifully dressed, with not only her beautiful gowns, but her sparkling eyes and precious smile attesting to her glamour. To whirl this dancing beauty around the large dance floor would constantly turn the head of almost everyone. I was the "man of the ball," showing off my Queen of the Ballroom Floor.

Ellie's stepfather, George Moon, was a World War I vet who had been gassed in France, for which he received about fifty dollars'

34

monthly compensation. This amount would not buy the gas for our cars these days, but it was what Ellie was raised on. It seems as though the hard times just really made Ellie and me appreciate all the more the nice things in life God was now helping us to achieve.

One evening, as I came home from work, my family met me at the car. They were so excited about an old farmhouse. So off we went to see this country charmer. It was a six-room stone house with a large front porch but no running water, no kitchen cabinets, etc. Only four walls, a ceiling, and a floor. This seemed disastrous after living in a new house for three or four years, but, you see, this was Ellie. She said, "We can make this our beautiful country home." Large, stately oak trees adorned the yard, and the rest was imagination for us.

Yes, we did it, with outdoor toilets and all. This persevering couple just sailed through the task at hand. Modern living was achieved in record time. Being so busy made the time just fly by. Many nights after the children were in bed asleep, Ellie and I would continue clearing the timber of the twenty-acre pasture, using the trees for making a rail fence around the circular driveway. These times seemed to make us closer and closer until we could almost read each other's mind. So many times, we were told we excelled as a couple. We magnified each other. It seemed Ellie and I were the stars of life; whatever beauty we possessed was from one another. It made us achieve perfection, if possible, whatever we did.

Sometimes, when we were dancing, the band would play a new dance like the cha-cha. The floor would clear because of the difficult steps, which left Ellie and me to show off. On conclusion the band, the dinner guests, and the waitresses would all applaud. What a thrill for me to have such a beautiful, talented partner. God's births in 1919–21 just made us that way. We were just one, as He ordained. We always would say, "Thank you, Sweet Jesus, for our happiness."

By this time, Ellie and I were middle-aged, so at dinner one evening I asked her if our third child was still on the agenda. She looked up at me with her beautiful Capricorn eyes and said, "C.E., I would just love to give you another son." God bless her heart, that's exactly what she did, eleven years after our first son, Don, was born. We named this baby Roy Mark Pittman. Roy was my father's name and Mark was a biblical name, which pleased my lady.

Patricia and Don loved their little brother. Now we were a full house, the Pittman five, a beautiful family. Ellie and I had achieved our goal and could say, "God, how truly great Thou art to pour out Your blessing upon this family."

A few years before, our neighbor Mr. Alcorn, who owned a soft ice cream store just a block from where we lived, always stopped to visit us as he walked to work, and in the course of conversation we talked about how lucrative this new kind of soft ice cream was. He always encouraged us to buy a franchise, which we did on West Highway 6 and 40 in Denver. I resigned from Sperry Vickers and put the country place up for sale, which put the Pittman five off to Colorado again.

Ellie's sister Mae rented us a house a few blocks from the new business. We enrolled our children back in school, and Ellie and I went to inspect our new adventure. We compared our contract with the location of the property and other pertinent facts that didn't jive as outlined!

We called for a meeting of company officials and, after a week or two, dissolved all previous agreements without penalty for either side. We called CJHS to see, if we came back to the country place, if Patricia could graduate there. (It was her senior year.) We were assured she could.

We called the realty company and asked to have the country place taken off the market. All was cleared and the Pittman five was on its way back. Before we left, Ellie's brother Bill and his wife, Helen, thought maybe we had financial problems because of our trouble with the soft ice cream business. They offered us their savings account if we needed it. God had given us so many precious people, and so grateful were we.

Once settled back into our home in the country, we would start all over again. As the days went by and our friends knew we were back, they would kid Ellie, saying, "Well, 'Mrs. Roosevelt,' not everyone can take their furniture on vacation." I think we all were happy to be back.

God always seemed to pick us up and put us in a more advantageous place, as I was now employed by the Sebastian Equipment Company in Joplin. This was to be my last employer other than myself. Mr. Ray Schurich and his wife, Marty, were longtime friends, and Ray was a splendid boss to me for many years to come.

One evening when the four of us were returning to Joplin after dinner in Pittsburg, Ray said, "What's that in the middle of the road?" It turned out to be white chickens that had been lost off a delivery truck. Everyone wanted to stop and get some to save them from certain death from the highway traffic. I think we put about five or six in the trunk of the car. What a crazy time we had.

Our son Mark was now in the Future Farmers group at school, so he and Ellie nurtured these chickens back to health. A few months later, at the Future Farmers fair, he won a blue-ribbon first prize. He and his mother were so proud; so were Patricia, Don, and I. The Schurichs could hardly believe that the highway chickens could ever be number one.

My friend and ex-boss Ray and I recently had lunch at a Chinese restaurant, and when I told him about this manuscript he was encouraging. Ray said that Marty, his wife, had asked him, "Why can't you be like C.E.? He is always so attentive to Ellie." I guess that kind of makes me a villain in our group of friends. However, Ray admitted that he would now prepare dinner on nights when Marty was volunteering her time at the medical center. When she gets back home after her work, she opens the door and asks, "Am I in the right house? It sure smells good." Ray would seat her at the table, light the candles, and do the sweet romantic things. Ray said Marty really enjoyed this, and he glanced at me as if to say, "C.E., thank you for being the friend you are."

Ray said the nicest thing a friend has ever said to me: "C.E., you and Ellie are just two special people. Romeo and Juliet were no match for you guys. In fact, I don't think anyone has ever been in love like you two." Now, are those loving words from this sweet man or not? God bless you, Boss!

A short time later my mother, Susie Alice, passed away. It's always such a difficult time when you lose your mother. It seems as though some of you goes with her. We laid her to rest in the Oronogo Cemetery, where my father and stepfather were buried. Ellie and I would always keep our mothers' resting places neat and brought in-season flowers to show our deep love for them. However, doing our best to live our lives as they taught us many years before was the most perfect tribute to those precious ladies. How beautiful God made our lives together.

Ray and Marty I think knew our sadness and invited us to take the train from Joplin to New Orleans for a few days. Gee, it was a big help to Ellie and me. We had such a good time going to almost every pub to hear different Dixieland bands until the wee hours. Breakfast time came so early, it seemed, and it was time to face the coffee, but grits and trimmings tamed it down.

One afternoon before returning to Joplin, we all sat to have our portraits sketched on the Bourbon Street sidewalk. Ellie and I asked the artist if we could have ours done together. He replied, "Surely, because you are special. I can tell." Most couples just have their sketches done separately. Almost thirty-five years later, this eighteen-inch-by-twenty-inch portrait still hangs on our master bedroom wall to remind us of good times with good friends.

This was the beginning of travel for Ellie and me. Besides working for Sebastian Equipment Company, I was a sales engineer for a high-speed tool manufactured in Chicago, a tungsten carbide manufactured in Milwaukee, and a high-speed form tool manufactured in Clearwater, Florida.

At this time, Ellie and I joined the Methodist church at Thirty-second and Pearl Street in Joplin. As we participated in the choirs, Ellie was asked to teach the first-grade class in Sunday school and I was asked to become a layleader. We both accepted with joy and pride. These days, months, and years were truly fun times.

One sad day Grandma Lilly went to heaven after a heart attack. This was such a hurtful time for my girl. I just hurt so deeply inside for her. As we stood in our kitchen, holding each other in our arms, I looked into Ellie's tear-filled eyes and could almost see her mourning soul. Silently I prayed that God would take this terrible hurt away. It broke my heart to see the sadness in those otherwise happy, loving green eyes of this beautiful lady. God just seemed to stay with us until we could bear this burden together. Of course, we visited the interment places of our mothers often.

In summertime, the Oronogo Cemetery was a shady place to walk, as Ellie and I tried to do two miles or so a day. At one end of our course was an artesian well with cold water overflowing into a stream. On a ninety-degree day, Ellie would take off her shoes and cool her feet while I did another fast mile. I would then drive the station wagon over to her, put the tailgate down, and pop open a cold drink. We would sit with our feet in the water. It was just so easy to find love with each other in any place we were. Taking our lunch to the cemetery was called "weird" by some people, but Ellie and I were the happy ones and this was truly known by all. God's love is like that, you know.

It was so enjoyable to work and travel with my girl, and one hot summer day when I came back to our motel in Tulsa, Oklahoma, early in the afternoon to see if Ellie and Mark were back from shopping, I found them in the swimming pool. They begged me to come in, and that's all it took. I ran in and changed, dashed to the diving board, and did a short jackknife into the water. I swam underwater to Mark, grabbing him by the legs and almost scaring him to death. My lady pressed her sweet lips on mine as if to say, "Gee, I'm glad you're here early."

A minute or so went by and I asked her if she wanted to have dinner in the dining room or on the plane. With a startled look on her face, she asked, "What plane?"

"The one going to Corpus Christi," I replied.

"I didn't know we were going to Corpus Christi," she said.

"Well, until an hour or so ago, I didn't either," I explained. "But let's get with it; plane time isn't too far away."

It was Mark's first plane ride, and he was nervous. But in a short time our plane was taxiing up to the Corpus Christi Air Terminal. We rented a car and drove to the oceanfront marina where the Sand & Sea Motel was located across the street. That evening, while Mark was in the pool, he learned to swim for the first time as Ellie and I relaxed on the pool patio with cold drinks. We were so proud of him, as he had tried so hard to accomplish this feat.

It was getting late and hunger pains set in and I said, "How lucky can you get? The noted Ship Ahoy Restaurant is just across the street." I went to get us carry-out shrimp and trimmings. Just as I got to the curb, they pulled the door blind that read: CLOSED. As persistent as I was, I pecked on the glass with a quarter. The waitress opened the door and I said, "I came to pick up our order of shrimp."

She asked my name and I told her, "Pittman, from Missouri." I told her we wanted three dozen shrimp, coleslaw, Texas toast, and seafood sauce. I'm so glad she didn't ask when the order was called in, because it wasn't, but she assumed so. In just a few minutes she returned with three white sacks full of good-smelling food. I paid the check and tipped that nice lady very well. Boy, did we have a late evening feast. We were having so much fun that going to bed on a full stomach didn't matter; we slept like logs.

The next three days were spent out on Padre Island, swimming, seashell hunting and just having a really good time. I could see that Ellie just loved the beach even if the temperature was almost one hundred degrees. We would take swims and ride the waves back to shore and make up little songs like: "You belong to me as the sand does to the sea! Here we belong, chasing the sun all day long!" All the time we were writing these words with a stick in the sand.

Love songs in our hearts came so easy, as did the love between us. My mind went back to our school days and the C & A Drive-In, where we promised each other a Hawaiian twenty-fifth anniversary vacation, which would come the following year. I was determined to pursue this promise to completion.

Ellie's sister Mary and her husband, Lynn, lived in Victoria, Texas, and had planned to meet us in Houston the next day. Ellie and I had arranged accommodations at the St. Francis Hotel for us all. We had such a nice visit with them and that evening was super also, as the Saint Louis Cardinals defeated Texas 5–4 at the Astro-dome.

Going to places we never thought possible was so romantic and fun times, places like the Alamo, the Royal Gorge, Carlsbad, the Golden Gage Bridge, the San Diego Zoo, the boardwalk, New Orleans, Saint Louis Arch, the Wrigley Building in Chicago, World Series baseball games, etc., places with star entertainers like George and Tammy Jones, Merle Haggard, Willie Nelson, Andy Williams, Liberace, Jim Nabors, Dinah Shore, and a host of others. All of this had seemed so far out of reach to this small-town couple.

Well, playtime was over for a while, so back home to work.

As we returned home, Ellie's brother George and his wife came to visit. George played the guitar well, and we had fun times singing along. He encouraged me to buy a guitar, and as the months rolled along, my fingers got tough enough so they didn't hurt anymore when I touched the strings.

Ellie had a pretty voice and could harmonize with me so well. Quickly we became the stars of our group. We would get together a couple times a month, especially in the winter, for a hoedown. Music was such a part of our life from the beginning. We even wrote songs together, and some they say were pretty good. "Why in the World" was our best, and at this writing, I cannot help believing that Ellie and I were writing this song about our future. And now the tears are so hard to hold back. Maybe at the end of this book will be a proper place to pen all the thoughts and all the words we put together. Then you'll see what perfect love God gave to Ellie and me. It's like we knew beforehand what the future held for us.

The winter was almost over. February was here and Hawaii was on my mind. I made arrangements with my boss to take off a couple of weeks at Valentine's Day. It seemed a better time to go to a warm place than June, which was when our twenty-fifty anniversary would be. I had made all the plans with the travel planning office, which gave me all the tickets and schedules for this promised trip.

I purchased new gold-colored luggage for Ellie and placed the tickets inside. That evening when I arrived home I took her to the car and opened the trunk. As she looked at the pretty luggage, she asked, "What's this?" I handed her the cosmetics bag and asked her to open it. When Ellie saw the Hawaii tickets she grabbed me around the neck, tears just flowing. All the time we were jumping up and down with joy while, in a trembling voice, she kept saying, "You didn't forget. You didn't forget. My love! My love! You didn't forget."

How could anyone not believe that almost twenty-nine years ago, when times were so hard during the depression years, God wasn't sitting right beside this small-town couple and listening to every word, for which we are so prayerfully thankful.

Our daughter, Patricia, and son Don were married by now, and Ellie's sister Mary agreed to care for Mark in our absence. I think Ellie shopped every day to supply us with the things she thought necessary. It was so wonderful to see her so very happy, just like when I came home from World War II.

When love really finds you, this love no one can explain. It causes so much joy, but then again, it can cause so much pain. At

42

this beautiful time of our lives together, we had only experienced the true-joy part; little did we know the pain was to come much later.

I had been to Hawaii twice while in the service of my country during World War II, but only by transport troopship.

Our day to leave was finally here, and as we awakened, to our dismay, we saw an ice storm had occurred in the night. We were so pumped up for this long-awaited vacation. We prayed the storm would not hinder our takeoff from the Joplin Airport. And it didn't!

We landed in Los Angeles with time to stretch our legs, have a cold drink, and get our flight info. When our number was called, Ellie looked up at me as only she could do and asked, "C.E., are you afraid to fly six hours over the Pacific Ocean?"

I assured this beautiful lady that as long as we were together nothing would scare me. I could just tell by her relaxed expression that was all she needed to hear. Board the plane we did.

The stewardesses were in Hawaiian dress, and Hawaiian music was piped into the cabin. It was just thrilling to see the happiness on my lady's face. When darkness had just proclaimed the day's end, we were landing on the Honolulu Airport runway. As we deplaned, we could hear our name being paged. We checked in at the flight desk, where a nice Hawaiian man and lady greeted us. The young man placed a beautiful lei around Ellie's neck and kissed her on the cheek as the young lady did to me. I looked over at Ellie and saw that she was having a difficult time holding back those happy tears that didn't hide the stars that sparkled in those beautiful green eyes.

The pretty Hawaiian couple didn't only greet us with their "Mahalo" (a greeting like "aloha"), but helped us with our luggage and a cab to the Halekulani Hotel. What a beautiful reception from these loving people. It just seemed to get us off on the right foot, because the next few days would just all seem like a love song.

The second night, we went to see Don Ho at Duke Kahonomaku's Supper Club. As we arrived, the place was packed and it looked like a thousand people were waiting for dinner and the Ho show. We had to take a bleacher-type seat. The arrangement was like a football stadium, with bleacher seats on both ends and candle-lit dining tables on the playing field. It was so exciting when the lights were dimmed to darkness. Ellie squeezed my hand so tightly, my fingers went to sleep. As a spotlight came on and a silhouette of Don Ho appeared on the bandstand, he started singing "Welcome to My World," one of our favorite songs by Jim Reeves. Mr. Ho and the band entertained us with some of their favorite songs, like "Tiny Bubbles" and "Hawaiian Love Song."

Mr. Ho got our attention by saying he would play a game with us if we would participate, and of course applause followed. He explained that he would call out a letter and anyone present from a state with a name beginning with that letter could yell out the state's name. Well, would you believe *M* was the first letter he called? Ellie jumped up from her seat yelling, "Missouri!" out so loud everyone, I'm sure, heard it. Mr. Ho sent an usher up to escort us to a stage across the dining room from him at a distance of maybe eighty or ninety feet. We were given a microphone as we arrived onstage. The nice Hawaiian introduced us to Mr. Ho as "Mr. and Mrs. C. E. Pittman, from Missouri, celebrating their twenty-fifth wedding anniversary."

Mr. Ho and all the guests applauded. As the noise ended, Mr. Ho said, "You are such a beautiful couple, are you sure you're not from Hollywood?" Much applause again as I looked over at Ellie while holding her hand. She turned to look at me and smiled just like the angel she was. Her beautiful smile told me this was a most exciting night for two poor little teenage kids from the Midwest. The C & A Drive-In seemed like yesterday.

Two other couples joined us onstage. The band played a slow dance number so we three couples could dance, but the space was rather small. Mr. Ho asked us to give back the microphone and said to us, "Mr. and Mrs. Pittman, from Hollywood, we have played music for you to dance by on our stage. Will you tell your friends back home you did this?"

Of course, our reply was, "Yes!"

"Well!" he exclaimed. "Now it's your turn to do something for us. Tell a joke, sing a song, or buy drinks for the house."

We told Mr. Ho we weren't good joke tellers and we didn't have the cash to buy the drinks, but we could sing a song by Jerome Kern that has filled our hearts with so much love and happiness since we had learned this song in 1938 while at the C & A Drive-In, where we promised each other that we would come to Hawaii on our twenty-fifth wedding anniversary.

The crowd applauded again. As quiet was restored, we told Mr. Ho the song we would like to sing was "All The Things You Are." He asked us, "What key?" and I replied, "Just about like I'm talking." Well! The band members fell out of their seats to the floor laughing; hysterical laughing and applause just seemed to come from everyone. All this fun just seemed to relax us. We told Mr. Ho his band was so good that they could pick up the key as we proceeded to sing. They did exactly that and we thought they made us sound pretty good. As we finished, the band and most of the crowd stood and applauded. Of course, Mr. Ho said to them, "You were supposed to save that for me!" and laugher rang out again.

Mr. Ho said, "I see why you didn't give us a key; there are six keys in that beautiful song, which you sang like pros."

As we were thanking Mr. Ho for this most wonderful time and leaving the stage, I saw a camera person coming up the aisle who took our photo. This person came to our seat and offered this picture for a price. Ellie and I were eager to have it, and all these years it has been in a group of eight pictures called "Happy Faces and Places of R. E. & C. E. Pittman." It hangs on the wall to remind us how wonderfully God blessed us with so much happiness. We were always so thankful for His watch over us.

The following day found us flying to Kona, Hawaii, for two days. It was so romantic: dinner by candlelight on the lanai (sort of

Ellie and C.E. singing at the Don Ho show (Hawaii).

Ellie and C.E., twenty-fifth wedding anniversary, 1966.

an outside porch) as the pretty music softly played and the sea waves came to share. It was so exciting for us. After dinner it was dancing under the beautiful Hawaiian star-lit sky, which cannot be described in a few simple words. The thrill of holding each other and whispering, "I love you," in each other's ears made it seem like a miracle was happening before our eyes, a dream of twenty-nine years ago come true.

Now, it's so difficult for me to hold back the tears of joy, for these most precious memories of yesteryear. Love is like that, don'tcha know.

The next day we were free to do as we wished. We went to the beach, where large volcanic rocks sheltered a small sandy eddy. We spent all day making a grass hut for shade and having a basket lunch. It seemed to be our private place, as only one couple passed us all day. It was like being alone in a world of your own, just a love story romance. As night fell on our precious day, we gathered our things and headed back to the Kona Inn for a nice shower and late dinner. We just had to stay awhile and dance. Some of the guests said, "You are a pretty dancing couple; you just flow together." Ellie was so graceful and beautiful, it was thrilling for me to show her off on the dance floor for everyone to see.

The next day we planned to take the tour bus to the volcano, waterfalls, lava tube, and fern tree gardens and on to Helo. Boarding time was 7:30 A.M. and when we arrived the only seats were in the far rear, where we plopped down. Ellie's shopping at home kept us in new clothes almost every day.

It was a beautiful Hawaiian morning and, like every morning, I picked flowers for Ellie's pretty hair. The flowers seemed to know that they enhanced her beautiful face.

As we sat waiting for our driver, we talked about the events of the day and night before. We were unaware our driver had arrived, and he turned up the microphone and said, "If the Hollywood couple in the rear will listen up, I will explain today's itinerary."

Beach at Hilo, Hawaii, 1966. Ellie sitting on the black sand.

Well, this Hollywood talk, twice in a week, was inflating our egos. But we knew it was just kind words from beautiful Hawaiian people. We just loved them all.

The day was fun: sightseeing, shopping for gifts having lunch, and just standing on the street corner. Ellie had saved several silver half-dollars, and when we spent them the natives were thrilled to get them, as they were rarely seen. At a nursery, we purchased a fern-tree Tiki god, ten inches in diameter and four feet tall, which they mailed home for us. It's standing in our garden, twenty-seven years later, and atop of it is a metal plaque given to us by my mother, Susie Alice, which reads: "The kiss of the sun for pardon, the song of a bird for mirth, one is nearer God's heart in a garden than anywhere else on Earth."

The Helo Hotel was old but very nice. Located downtown, it was nice for shopping. Sunday buffet, after church, was fabulous, with an ice sculptor and all; he carved out a four-foot swan in no time. The food was excellent, but I had had enough ice for one day. It seemed everyone had iced tea, and you know the sound of iced tea stirrers.

Ellie remarked, "C.E., you're getting old when you can't stand noise from happy people." She explained that almost everyone is happy when they are eating. Of course, that was a shot in fun.

Next day, Aloha Airlines flew us to Maui. We rented a car and drove up to Hana, a small town where Charles A. Lindbergh loved to visit so much he was buried there. We enjoyed the beautiful drive, about one hundred miles round-trip. We didn't flow with the crowd on our tour because they didn't seem to like the offbeat places (the real Hawaii) as Ellie and I did. The local people were so sweet and kind, which fueled the thought that God was everywhere. We always thanked Him for the lovely experience.

We had dinner on our way back to Maui at a roadside Japanese café that served us veal and red fish cooked in olive oil with Japanese veggies and tea—just excellent.

The following day we went back to Honolulu for one more day in God's beautiful place. It was sad, because we wanted to stay a while longer, but plans didn't allow that. A few days before, we had seen a "cook-it-yourself" steak house we decided to try for dinner. What an experience. You pay up front and the cashier gives you a hot baked potato, a raw sirloin steak, plate, and utensils; salad and trimmings were in the dining room, which had about eight charcoal grills. You muscle up and plop your steak on the grill. What real togetherness. However, everyone was having so much fun.

It was such a tender steak it surprised me. The laughter and fellowship took our minds off of our departure the following day. We went to bed early, as our plane time was early also. We just couldn't get to sleep, talking about the most enjoyable times of the past ten days. Ellie put her arms around my neck and whispered in my ear, "You know, C.E., this is the first time in the past twenty-five years I felt as though I had you all to myself, alone. I thank you, my darling, for the thrill of a promise from our teen years that seemed almost impossible to come true. Isn't God wonderful to us? I'm sure He will see us safely home."

We boarded the early plane after customs. The beautiful Hawaiian music seemed to soothe our sadness for leaving this beautiful time together behind. Little did we know it would remain in our hearts forever.

Our plane took off and, after reaching altitude, seat belts were off and a champagne breakfast was on. The PA system came on and the first song was a longtime favorite of ours, "Impossible Dream." Ellie looked over at me, took my hand, and kissed my fingers with tears of joy streaming down her beautiful face. Instantly I stood up, gently led her to the aisle, and held her closely while we danced cheek-to-cheek, tear-to-tear. But the smiles we gave to each other would not wash away because of the love God had put there Himself. When the music ended, applause came from most everyone, but we had become unaware of them. It kind of embarrassed us, but the stewardess came on the PA system and remarked, "Didn't we just experience love in full bloom? Thank you."

We settled down and enjoyed a safe trip home to Joplin, where we enjoyed sharing the excitement of the last ten days with family and friends.

4

Sometimes it seemed as if our children were a little awed at our abilities and the ease with which happiness came to Ellie and me. So very often we were told we could pass for brother or sister after they were in their thirties. Really being happy and truly in love will do that, dont'cha know.

Sometimes now, as I look back to yesterday, it seems as though Ellie and I were almost misfits in our world. When we were planning our itinerary for another Hawaii vacation, we promised to go to the leper colony island of Molokai. So many times we were asked, "Why there?" We really didn't know ourselves at the time.

Aloha Airlines had left off all of its passengers at Kona, Maui, Helo, and Hawaii, and that left Ellie and me alone to be the last to disembark at Molokai. We found out later why we had to see this most beautiful place. As I remember, the Hawaiian cliffs overlooking the leper colony are among the highest above any ocean. If there is a tranquil place on this Earth, here it was before our eyes. The reefs went out to sea almost as far as the eye could see. This caused the soft breakers to chase each other to the beach where the colony had been built years ago. Being up so high in ginger groves above this magnificent scene was like watching a silent movie. Here we were alone in the world that seemed to have forsaken us. The soft Hawaiian sea breeze seemed to urge us to a most precious embrace, and as we looked into each other's eyes, it seemed God was telling us this was a most special place for two of the most special people so in love. It was as though God was giving us an award for our love affair. Was this true love or what?

As the years rolled by, on some holidays like Mother's Day, birthdays, and Christmas, Ellie wouldn't receive the generosity of gifts from our family, as if she were a forgotten person. However, I would do my best to make up for the omissions.

This sweet lady never complained, though inside the tormenting question from her to herself was, I'm sure, *Why?* I was blessed with the same treatment when it became my turn to be disappointed. However sad it was, we could always hold each other in such a loving embrace and be forgiving and ungrudgeful. This took a lot of power from above. I'm sure you can imagine that.

God always seemed to be there when the trials of life were weighing so heavy on the soul. "What a close and dear Friend we found in Jesus," was always Ellie's remark.

She would cut out a poem from the paper or magazine and put it in a place where, later on, she would discover it again and it seemed to always lift her spirits. One such poem, by Virginia Katherine Oliver, was "The Diary of Life".

"The Diary of Life" prompts all who read it to take heed of how we live because someday down the road we'll all have to look back at our lives and account for not just the good we have done, but the bad, as well.

You see, it behooves all to address their actions and replace the bad with good so when the Book of Life is opened before us the moment will be tranquil.

What a few words of advice. We all know, I'm sure, human perfection was only for Jesus Christ, the Son of God, but this poem encourages us to diligently live our lives toward this goal.

Our 1969 Valentine's Hawaii vacation did not begin well, as our plane from KC to LA had a fire in one engine while we were over the Grand Canyon. About three hundred people were aboard, and the pilot informed us we would make an emergency landing at Las Vegas. I could see Ellie was fighting the fear as we held hands. I told her, "Everything will be OK."

A young lady to my left asked, "How do you know?"

As I explained to her, she held my arm like Ellie. As the airport came in sight, we could see firemen in white suits foaming the runway for us to land. Here was God again, with His hands on the controls, giving us a safe landing, which prompted a round of applause from everyone. When my wrists and arms were free, fingernail marks were visible on each side. I just smiled inside and said, "Thank you, Jesus."

All this caused us to be off-schedule; instead of landing in Hawaii at six in the afternoon, we landed in the wee hours of the morning. Our luggage didn't get off the plane but went to Tokyo. Mr. Lee, the Halekulani Hotel manager, was concerned about us because of the late hour. This nice man waited up for us and escorted us to our condo, which had baskets of fruit, cookies, and a bottle of wine. He had toiletries sent to us, and we just slept without our PJs.

We received our luggage back the next afternoon. We soon forgot the hassle and good times were here again. One day, we drove over past Hickam Field, which had been one of the main targets for the Japanese planes on December 7, 1941. As we drove maybe three miles down the road, I said, "Sweetheart, let's have lunch here on this beautiful beach."

It was like having a private beach all to ourselves. We just had to go for a swim before lunch, and as we were having a good time, I noticed a helicopter flying along the beach, the people waving at us. So, being friendly, we waved back. The next trip past us they flew really low, so we could read a sign they held in the door, which said: "Sharks. Get Out." Boy, did we get out of there. It made us so nervous we could hardly eat our lunch. The following morning a shark notice was front-page news in the Honolulu paper.

We arrived back home again. The old country place had a large front porch we remodeled by bricking the cement floor, erecting large white pillars, and putting up a five-foot porch swing. Many evenings before dinner, when Ellie knew I had had a hard day at work, she would serve the kids dinner and when I got home a fresh pot of coffee was ready. We would take our cups to the porch swing and talk about each other's day. Boy! How she could "make the world go away" for me.

Ellie taught me how to love, how to be a best friend, how to be a faithful partner, and how to be as good a father as she was a mother. I also learned how to be a good husband and to love God with all my heart. She was so exciting to my life, and God saw to it that time never tarnished the sparkle that He had put between us. The gleam in our eyes attested to our vibrant life.

Our children helped us to have a twenty-fifth wedding anniversary open house on June 14. They made it a fun day with family and many dear friends. By this time the remodeling of our old country place was in full swing. The house was furnished in beautiful taste as only Ellie could do. The acreage was cleared and a spring-fed lake was finished and stocked with fish. After a twenty-seven-foot-by-eighteen-foot family room with fireplace, red sculptured carpet, and thirty-six windows was completed, Ellie had said to me, "C.E., I told you we could make this our beautiful country place." No one could deny that.

[Ellie, like her mother, loved to fish, and fortunate were we to have a large river, called Spring River, close by. We purchased a mobile home and leased a fishing lot to set it on. The ensuing years at our fishing and boat dock were really fun. Ellie would get so excited when we caught a large catfish (forty or fifty pounds) on a line tied to a tree limb.

Ellie's brother owned a bait shop, and one time he gave us three oversized goldfish, about ten inches long, for bait. They were so big for bait that we didn't have much faith in them. But lo and behold, our last bait would bring us lunch, maybe.

As we approached the line, tied to a tree limb, it sprang into action. There were so many logs under the water we had to turn off the boat motor and paddle up to the fishing line. All this time we were planning our strategy to capture this lunker of a fish. Years of experience told us he was very big, so Ellie got on her knees in the boat and positioned her dip net as I handled the fishing line.

Our first attempt to land him was futile. However, we got to see his size. Boy! His head was the size of a large dishpan! We

A country Christmas, 1975. Ellie and C.E. in their new family room, by the fireside.

thought he weighed maybe sixty pounds or so. Our next effort also failed, as he broke the hook swivel from the line on his last surge for freedom, splashing water all over Ellie and me.

Oh, how much she wanted that fish. It would have been a record size for our locale. As I looked over at her, she just sat back in the seat and cried. I sat there with her as we embraced until we gained control again. I comforted her by saying, "Sweetheart, just think of the stories we can tell about the big one that got away, and only we and God know the truth."

That brought a smile from my lady. Days, months, and years later we still thought he would come back to that fishing line. Fishermen are like that, don'tcha know.

Ellie's brother George and I went to KC Veterans Hospital for a checkup, and they found I had plaque in my arteries that needed attention. My darling was so upset about this, but as always, reasoning together about this calmed the fears. I was off to Columbia Veterans Hospital, where heart surgery was performed. I was told about 75 percent of vets going there for surgery backed out and went home. Fear, I guess.

Before going to surgery I had Ellie call our oldest son, Don, to come and be with her that day. The bypass open-heart surgery was a success, and about a week or so later we were on our way home. Ellie said, "Thank you, Sweet Jesus," almost every mile of the way.

Oh, she was so glad it was over, because this operation was in its infancy and results were not always 100 percent. But God made it perfect for us because, at this writing, it has been twenty years and I walk two and a quarter miles a day in twenty minutes and do forty pushups every morning after I get out of bed from a good night's sleep. No one can say God is not good.

By this time, winter was at hand, which made it too cold to walk even a mile a day, so Ellie drove us to Clearwater for the winter. While going to dinner one evening, we saw Evelyn, Joe, and Smitty, who were friends from Joplin years ago, and that was a nice visit. The days went by fast, and Ellie and I were glad, because the humidity was so bad.

When springtime in Missouri came, we were back to our houseboat. We had sold our mobile home and dock because of the uncertainty of the future. But that didn't stop the fishing fever at all. By now, I could look into Ellie's pretty green eyes and see all her fear was gone, which made me say a "Thank You," also.

5

A short distance downstream from our old fishing place was a private park for houseboats. They were one-room efficiencies sitting on the water and floated by Styrofoam logs. We picked out one of the boats that looked the best and began trying to purchase it from the owner. We did so in about a month. Being able to buy this relaxing place prompted us to think seriously about retiring. This was accomplished in a few weeks. God had provided us with the necessary means to do this comfortably.

We had heard so many stories about how difficult life became after retiring, that being under each other's feet, so to speak, wasn't so great. But this never caused a second thought, because we never knew anyone that was blessed with our special kind of love, which could have only come from heaven. Knowing that as truth, the next fifteen years of retirement with my girl were just perfect.

Our first week at the houseboat we met our next-door neighbor, who was a divorced man about sixty years old. His name was Francis. He was destined to become a very good friend to Ellie and me.

We noticed crawfish under our walkway, which ran from the bank to the houseboat. We got the dip net and tried to catch them. I fell off the walkway into the water while holding a net full of crawfish above my head. We laughed up a storm as Ellie knelt down on the carpeted walkway and kissed me smack on my wet lips and face.

Many months later, on a hot day, Francis came over to our picnic table, sipping on a cold beer, and related to us about those crawfish and the kiss. He said, "You two are unbelievable. Here you are married over forty years and you act like it's your honeymoon."

That was Ellie and me, but we never gave it a thought. I guess it just came so easily and natural. True love is like that, don'tcha know.

Many years later, when Francis and his wife reconciled, he said to her, "I want to be just like the Pittmans." They are always happy and loving to each other now. They never fuss or fight or use harsh words.

As the summer progressed, we built a boat and swimming dock, which was nice for the hot days when we couldn't go to KC and see a Royals baseball game. Ellie was an excellent "fisherperson." We would catch more fish from our houseboat dock than most fishermen in boats. Four-to-six-pound black bass off the walkway weren't to be sneezed at.

For years now, every Friday had been our date day. Sometimes we would go to our houseboat early in the afternoon before the others would come with their families. Ellie would bring the tape player and our favorite tapes, and we would fix ourselves a table on the front porch of the houseboat and dance the afternoon away. Boats would go by and honk as if they were giving their approval. It was nice not to have the smoke and stale air that are always present in a club. Sometimes I would even give Ellie a little gift of some kind, which always put the sparkle in her beautiful green eyes.

It seemed so strange we didn't like fish to eat but loved to catch them. We always filleted them for friends and family. Mrs. Fro, our landlord, just loved for Ellie to bring her these nicely packaged fillets.

One Saturday morning, we caught a fourteen-pound catfish and Ellie wanted to clean it for our daughter, Pat. I talked Ellie into letting me show it to Pat's kids, who were about ten years old at the time. When we arrived at Pat's house, Ellie talked to them in the yard as I took the catfish to the back door and put the fish in the bathtub halfway full of water.

As they came into the house, I asked to wash my hands and they followed me to the bathroom and as the light was turned on that big fish gave a flop that sprayed all of us with water. It half-scared them to pieces. Of course, I had to mop up. It was worth it to see the grandkids enjoy it.

I can't say as much for the time we caught six or eight large bullfrogs (in season) and took them to Ellie's sister Iva, who loved frog's legs. She wasn't home, so we tied the frogs to her kitchen chair with fishing line. When she came home that night those crazy frogs were jumping all around under the table. Iva ran to a neighbor and said someone was in her kitchen. When she learned what we had done she said she could have killed us (jokingly, of course).

Ellie was the baby of a family of ten children, eight girls and two boys. What a sweet bunch they were. They were my brothers and sisters as they were hers, as was her mother, Grandma Lilly. When God blesses you with two families in one lifetime, as He did me, "Oh how sweet it is," as Jackie Gleason would say.

Our *Joplin Globe* daily newspaper had run a cartoon-type little boy and girl with cute sayings about "Love is . . ." One such cartoon shows the little boy putting worms on the girl's fishing hook while she holds a hanky to her nose—now that's love. Ellie always cut out and saved these kinds.

One birthday, Ellie gave me a nice Larson fiberglass boat and seventy-five horsepower motor. It was so nice, with seats back to back and a convertible top. It was fifteen feet long and six feet wide; what a stable craft.

On a warm, beautiful, starlit night we would take a slow midnight ride to cool off. If Ellie's tape was playing one of our songs I would stop and tie up to a tree limb and we would dance the song away. What happy, loving times we had. Love was always so fresh and new and as exciting as our first week of marriage. Here we were in our sixties; what a wonderful life we had as this feeling continued into our seventies.

Since our retirement, we would spend January and February

and sometimes March in Corpus Christi, to be able to walk on the beach instead of in the snow and cold. We were fortunate to have a condo with about two and a half miles of beach, which gave us a very nice walk. We found out that leaving a month's deposit would reserve the same condo that we liked for next winter, which we always did. Ours faced the south, and the view was the harbor bridge and large ship lines to the docks. Across the bay were high-rise buildings downtown, which, at night, were a beautiful sight with all the different-colored lights. It was so romantic when the waves came ashore gently, with beautiful reflections in the seawater.

Strolling hand in hand on a moonlit night seemed to put us in another world. I feel so sorry for ones who can't take God's beautiful creations and feel He made them especially for them. That's how lovers feel, don'tcha know.

This time was always a nice winter break. On Sunday morning we would go to the First Methodist Church on the bay, relishing the word of God and enjoying the beautiful choir music. Of course, the Sunday brunches were so different from Missouri food, but they were excellent.

On Christmas and New Year's Eve we would take off our footwear and wade the surf up to our knees, and some years that was cold. As most everyone by now knew us, we were called "winter Texans."

Our condo had couples from Nebraska, Kansas, Oklahoma, Arkansas, and Missouri housed close together, so we became friends. Some Sundays after church, we would have our own brunch or buffet with everyone pitching in. On special holidays, we took turns having really fun parties. After winter was over in the Midwest, all were homeward bound. We always corresponded until the next snow flurry came and we all went south. There are only two of us left from this group of lovely winter friends. God was good to give us all of them.

The condo rent was $275 per month at the beginning, but our

last stay cost $1,400.00. That put most of us back in the cold Midwest winters.

We always enjoyed large, beautiful houseplants, such as Hawaiian ti plants, crotons, and ferns. Our oldest son, Don, enjoyed gardening as we did, so he cared for them each winter we were away. Boy, was he happy when his mother and father stayed home for the winter.

Our son Roy Mark's son was crazy about his "Grandmother Ruby," as he called her. (Ruby was Ellie's first name.) Before he was school age sometimes we would keep him with us for weeks. He was such a sweet boy and loved us as we loved him. He always wanted me to play the guitar so he could sing, "Mama, Don't Let Your Babies Grow Up to Be Cowboys," which we taught him in about a week.

Ellie even bought him a cowboy hat. Those were sure precious times, which now are yesterday's memories. Often we would take him to dinner with us. When about three years old, he told the waitress, "This is my Grandma Ruby," about twenty times. I always seated Ellie at the table and kissed her gently on the lips before seating myself. The waitress said, "This fellow likes you, I think. Also, he's a gentleman. Not too many men do that anymore."

It was so natural to be polite and loving with Ellie, opening car doors, holding her hand while crossing the street. Just little things seemed so big to other people, like helping each other on with our coats. Being attentive and sweet to each other was our life. No one could deny that; that's what made our life together so beautiful and happy.

Our grandson Michael, the "Grandma Ruby" boy, loved to walk with me, and one day he stopped still and watched a robin fly to land on a fence post. He looked up at me and said, "Grandpa, the next time you talk to Jesus, ask him to make me fly like that bird." Michael's thinking amused me, as he was just four years old.

We had our washer and dryer on a closed-in back porch. One day, Michael came up the stairs and said through the screen door,

"Grandma Ruby, I'm going to Taco Bell you," and he pushed the doorbell button and we all laughed together. He was some cute boy.

Ellie wasn't a morning person, especially before coffee. When we first awakened, I loved to put my arm around her, kiss her on the neck, and say, "Good morning, darling. I love you for all day." She could hardly mutter, "Me, too." I didn't need words to explain her love for me; I just needed her to hold my hand even as we slept, as we did almost every night all our married life. Hands can hold a multitude of love. Love is like that, don'tcha know. God just seemed to keep us so young, physically, mentally, and spiritually.

My breakfast chore was pouring orange juice, fixing an orange or grapefruit, and setting the breakfast table, after which I was out of the house to get the morning paper, look over our pretty yard, and thank Jesus for another beautiful day. Soon, I could hear a peck on the window and, with her precious smile, Ellie would gesture with her cup that coffee was ready. In the summer months, when I stepped inside she would remark, "C.E., your roses are so beautiful this morning." She could see them from the kitchen windows. I just loved to make her happy. Like every morning for fifty-three years, this was the beginning of another beautiful day together.

On our shopping days for groceries and drug supplies, I would slip away to the cosmetic counter and buy her perfume, etc. One day, the lady clerk asked, "Would your lady friend like something new?" She showed me a bottle that cost about thirty-five dollars, which I took. After I paid, she said, "Your lady friend must like expensive things."

I just replied, "Yes."

This went on for a year or two, and I never told her any different. Isn't that awful?

Ellie and I enjoyed giving to each other. The last twenty-five years or so that I worked, Ellie would go to the men's store in Webb City, Missouri, and purchase me the nicest sports jackets, ties, shirts, etc. My colleagues would remark, "You always look like you just stepped out of the band box," whatever that means. I hope it's nice.

Shopping together was always enjoyable, but it was necessary for me to do upkeep work on the house and yard, so Ellie would go without me sometimes. It wouldn't be long before here she came, saying, "C.E., please wash up and come with me." And that I would gladly do. Just being together was so special for us. Doing so from 1937 to 1994, we never lost that loving feeling.

Her graceful beauty just seemed to be timeless. She truly was a Rembrandt subject or a Da Vinci "Mona Lisa." But in my eyes, they were no match for this beautiful lady. Remember the old sayings "stop and smell the roses" and "slow down and enjoy life"? Well, Ellie and I always had time for that, holding hands, taking time to love and to look so deeply into each other's eyes. We could almost see our souls and hear the beautiful music we made together. What a miracle of love God worked in us. This bubbling over of happiness prompted us to always be singing, whether we were walking, riding, or working. Of course, the love songs in our early life just kept coming and the sparkle in our eyes grew even brighter.

Every new song would make our feet want to dance in the kitchen, where, down through the years, we taught each other new dance steps that made us show off a little the next time we went out.

As one gets older, time just seems to recede. My brother Howard, sister Melba, and sister Ruth had passed away. Just after this time, Ellie's brother George passed away. This was very hard for Ellie, because George and she had grown up together, as all the other brothers and sisters were much older and married by then. God was always with Ellie and me, wiping away our tears of sadness and giving us the understanding and comfort we needed. Day by day and night by night the pain began to fade somewhat. I suppose life's greatest tragedy is the loss of family and dear friends. As life goes on, these unhappy events intensify and cause one to begin to get his house in order, and that isn't a small task if done correctly. Of course, giving one's self to God would be first on the list, and also preplanned burial to eliminate painful family efforts at such a sad time.

In George Straight's song "In All the World," he tells his lady that no one can love her as truly as he can. Then I would spoil it by adding, "from this little old country boy from Oronogo, 'Mo,' how much he loves you, you'll never know." Isn't that awful? But it would make us laugh so hard. Good times with Ellie and me were so simple. That's what kept us young.

It's funny how music can stimulate joy between lovers. To elaborate on this thought, for Valentine's Day, 1993, Ellie gave me a Valentine card with a picture of a piano and rose bud laid across the sheet music. Inside, the verse read: "You are my music, you are the one who makes my heart dance just by being near. When we are apart you stay with me like a love song I play over and over in my mind. You are my music, you are my Love." The card was signed: "Happy Valentine's Day, Sweetheart C.E., All my love, Ellie."

Little did I know this would be the last Valentine my sweetheart would give to me. And at this moment I must muster all my strength to slow the flow of tears from this broken heart, to reflect back on words and thoughts we had together many times, which I had etched on a gold necklace: "God watch between me and thee while we are apart one from the other," and He never failed us one time. Ellie would always say, "Thank you, Sweet Jesus. Thank you."

When we were in Hawaii, every evening professional entertainers would perform for free on Waikiki Beach. One such time, three Hawaiian ladies sang a new song they had just written only days before. It went something like this: "If I get to heaven and you're not there, I'll carve your name on the golden stairs." I'm sure that's what my Ellie is doing right now. The next line of the song was "He [God] picked you out from all the rest because He knew I'd love you best." So many times in our life together, Ellie lifted me up almost to heaven, but always gently let me down; she just seemed to keep my world slowly going round and round.

We were older now and years passed more swiftly. It just seems like yesterday when Ellie's father, Bill Roller, suffered a stroke that paralyzed him on the left side, which put him in a rest home for about sixteen years before his death. Wouldn't you know this beautiful Christian lady would take our children to see him every week and would buy him the things he needed? He would say, "I'll pay you." And her reply was: "Next time, Dad." I know God loved her for these sweet ways.

I think our love for each other was so fulfilling that all else was trivial. We could almost vanquish each other's problems and hurts by holding each other's hands and just starting walking slowly and talking quietly while looking into each other's eyes.

Not long ago, the Glaser Brothers had a hit song titled, "Loving Her Was Easier." That was me with Ellie; she was so easy to be with all during our life together. She really was so easy to love. I would like to think I was also. Ellie made sure that I knew that many times in our fifty-odd years of marriage. I just loved it when Ellie would say, "You know, C.E., you're my guy."

One December day, while Ellie and I were fishing in Corpus Christi Bay for redfish, she quietly said to me (as if she wasn't sure she wanted me to hear), "C.E., would you like to move back to the city, as twenty acres is a lot of work at our age." I had no answer off the top of my head. That evening at dinner, we talked about it at length. All our children were married, and it was more property than we needed.

Well, two years later we hadn't found our place yet. One day, while looking at real estate ads, Ellie said, "Get your coat. Let's go." She seemed so excited and off we went to see this city jewel. It was just that: two stories, full basement, two or three lots with stately oak trees, two-car garage, a twenty-six-foot-by-twenty-two-foot summer house, and paved driveway. No question, we purchased it from the original owners, who had built this lovely cobblestone house sixty years ago. It was still in mint condition. Close to us were the North Park Mall, many supermarkets, etc. Later we came to find out the most coveted thing was such very nice neighbors. Before we bought this home, we would drive up the driveway and park by the summer house, turn out the lights, and just watch the neighborhood. They have never said, but I bet they thought we were thugs meeting to steal something, as the house was empty.

This new home was easy, but giving up the old country place was so very difficult. Disposing of thirty-five years of stuff was a challenge. On our last day in this lovely place, Ellie and I walked all over the pasture holding hands and reminiscing on all the love and good times we and our family had shared through the years. Our eyes teared until we could hardly see to walk. Even with such sadness, we could look up to heaven and say, "Thank you, Sweet Jesus, for giving us all the happiness we most surely enjoyed here. We hope you will bless us the same in our new home and bless the new owner of our country place, Route 3, Box 456." I think this was the first time we really realized that nothing is forever except eternal life with God.

The moving van came the next day, and we spent our first night in the city in thirty-five years. The next day was Black Thursday, 1987, when the stock market fell. It scared Ellie, as we hadn't even sold our country place yet. The realty company wanted to list it, but I convinced Ellie we could sell it ourselves.

Here came God again, as two days later we did a good job of selling, as God was our Teacher. We saved several thousand dollars, which helped us to do some remodeling on our new house. Ellie was so good at beautifying every room with excellent taste.

By now, wintertime was at hand in Joplin and our first snow in December 1987 fell gently in the night. I awakened in early morning and, to my surprise, the ground was covered with about ten inches of snow. I awakened Ellie, as she always enjoyed seeing this sight before animals and cars made their tracks. It was too early for my sleepyhead girl, as she hopped back into bed. I got a drink of water and came back and knelt beside Ellie and whispered, "Let's go to Corpus Christi today."

Boy, out she bounded, and by noon we were leaving the city limits of Joplin and the cold days of winter behind. As in other winters past, we had the best time being together, holding hands and leaving our footprints in the sand. In my heart, I knew she belonged to me as the sand does to the sea, never to part. She smoothed my life as God orders the sea to smooth the sand on the beach.

On shopping days, Ellie would try to enlarge her teddy bear collection by finding bears she didn't have. By the time winter was over, the car trunk would reflect her success. These little critters would put the sparkle of joy in her beautiful eyes, and that was a great joy for me.

When we lived in the old country place, Ellie's stepfather would come every day, as Ellie would give him milk, eggs, etc., and always pie or cake. She was so good to him, cleaning his house, doing a sinkful of dishes, and grocery shopping with her own money.

When George died he didn't leave a will, and his nearest relatives, who never gave him charity or a kind word, took all his belongings and property without any consideration for his loving stepdaughter of twenty-five years. I knew in her heart that she would have liked to have had some of the little things that were her mother's and George's together. What little money was involved didn't interest Ellie at all. It makes you realize how selfish some people are. If we only knew that hearts aren't made to break; they are made to love, as the Holy Book teaches. "So be ye kind one to the other tender hearted, forgiving one another" (Eph. 4:32); "There for love is the fulfilling of the law" (Pss. 13:10); "Live joyfully with the wife whom thou lovest all the day" (Eccles. 9:9); and "She opened her mouth with wisdom and her tongue is the law of kindness" (Prov. 3:26). This was my lady, so loving, kind, and tenderhearted. Her wisdom guided the Pittman family on the happy road of life for over fifty years. She always depended upon the faith of prayer to supply her never-ending love and understanding, even in the darkest days. How precious was the gift of this special lady to me.

Up to now I haven't mentioned many friends, which isn't an oversight. Friends are such special loving people, and we were blessed with so very many. It would take another book to name them all and to relate their special times with us.

Ellie loved to host parties for them. She was always so beautifully dressed, and the food and tables were just as pretty and tasteful. What a joy to help her prepare this fun time, because it was sweet time with my lady. My job was to fix the nuts and fruits and veggies.

Of course, I was good at scouring pots and pans, and dish-washing was my daily chore. Ellie would always say, "Use the auto-washer." My retort was: "How else can I get my fingernails clean?" Instantly, there came the floured hands to my cheek. Ghastly, don't you think?

We made fun of most everything. We came into this world with this gift of life, and we traveled down life's road in our own way. However, we who take the ever-elusive life of true love on this journey are but a very few. We take this blessing at life's end back to heaven from whence it came in the first place. As my Ellie would say: "Thank you, Sweet Jesus."

I cannot recall a time that we didn't kiss each other upon leaving or arriving home. It was as if to say, "I'll miss you, sweetheart, while I'm gone," or "I'm so glad to feel your lips on mine again." Love was such a powerful mood to us. *Webster's Dictionary* doesn't have the words to explain this feeling. Together we could turn a cloudy, gloomy day into sunshine; a sad day into a happy day; a dark and gloomy night into a star-filled, heavenly adventure of love. People who visited our home would most always say, "We can just feel the love touching us in your home," as they looked at photos, beautiful flowers, candles, and the like. Romance was so evident.

Ellie enjoyed showing off her teddy bear critters, a collection of about one hundred, and she knew their names every one. Her Christmas collection was of beautiful figurines. I loved to see her explaining them to guests as her eyes attested to her joy. I think the joy Ellie obtained from little things, like her china dolls, was due to her not having little-girl things as a small child. She was only two or three years old when her father, Bill Roller, left her, her brother George, and her mother (Grandma Lilly). This caused her mother to find work at a potato chip factory to maintain their livelihood. Ellie and George told us that their father only came to see them once or twice. One Christmas he gave them one orange apiece.

Grandma Lilly was a holy person. God put within her heart the kind of love that made these three friends for life as well as making her a precious mother. Grandma Lilly was so proud of Ellie, her beautiful daughter, and in our young life as teenagers I'm sure her prayers were a large part of God's will to take over our lives together from the beginning to the end. Somehow she seemed to know God had determined I and her daughter would be man and wife. One could see the love in her eyes when we came to visit. When life has been so wonderful and sweet, flashbacks of faces and places and precious memories happen so often when our days become shorter. I think now of the fun Ellie and I had with our three children and how we kind of grew up together. Every day was happy times.

Going to church on Sundays was special, and eating out for lunch was a big deal also. Sometimes we took a long Sunday afternoon ride or played croquet, badminton, or baseball, all the summer games.

Winter games were just as much fun. We had snowball fights, erected snowmen, and went ice-skating and sledding down Churchwell's Hill, a block from the country place. The gradual

71

slope was about a quarter-mile and going down was great, but the trudging uphill was not so much fun. When tiredness set in back home we would go for popcorn or caramel corn and TV for a while.

There were the tough times, too, like homework lessons. Ellie and I helped when needed. And then there was teeth brushing and beddy-bye time, during which we would listen to their prayers and kiss them goodnight. Silently, in our hearts, we thanked the Good Lord for these, our precious ones.

Aren't close families growing up so exciting? It made Ellie and me like kids ourselves. Sometimes, when the bright moonlight was on the white snow, Ellie and I would see if our three angels were asleep and then get the sled and slide down Churchwell's Hill on a very cold winter night. The quiet, brisk air was so romantic with Ellie. I can remember one time saying to her, "See all those bright stars? They twinkle just like your pretty eyes when you're happiest. I hope I can always make you happy and proud. I love you with all my heart. Jesus surely picked you out from all the rest because he knew I'd love you best."

She just smiled so cute and said, "C.E., you're kidding this girl."

Then a warm embrace caused us to fall off into the snow and we ran for home.

Christmas evening was a big thing at our country place. Unwrapping gifts and baking cookies and other sweets were so much fun. These precious times with our children didn't end when they got married; they just got better because then we had grand-children.

When Ellie's brothers' and sisters' families would come, our old country place bulged with people. We have slept six or eight on the floor many times. They all liked to come to our house. I guess the country enhances the Christmas spirit. Of course, the delicious food prepared by Ellie was an attraction by itself. She would display all the delicacies, from salads to main course and dessert, that make hunger pains go wild: ham, turkey, and rolled sirloin roasts; dips and chips, veggies and fruit plates; cakes and pies that were as appealing to the eyes as to the stomach, all displayed on a festive tablecloth with matching napkins and fresh flowers. It truly was a Christmas banquet. I never ever felt that Ellie got the praise she deserved for her perfect efforts to keep our family close with these wonderful get-togethers. However, never a complaint from this precious lady.

The last Christmas get-together, each male was to bring a man's gift and each lady, likewise, brought a gift for a woman. Before everyone departed for their respective homes, Ellie and I sent one lady and one man to pick out a gift for themselves. Ellie and I went last and all the ladies' gifts were gone, but Ellie never let on. I didn't know this until all the guests were gone. My gift was a fancy honey jar filled with the best honey, so we just shared that with each other. Honey was one of Ellie's favorite foods, so this put a twinkle in her eyes. I kidded her that honey was what made her so sweet.

We cleaned up the mess, stacked dishes in the sink, donned our jackets, and went for a midnight walk on the cold winter Christmas Eve night. We reassured ourselves that like us, everyone had had a good time.

When we returned home and came to the door, I thanked Ellie for this beautiful evening together, like I did when we were kids dating. I put my hands inside her open jacket, and her sweet-smelling perfume reminded me of years ago, the first time I smelled this lovely lady and felt the warmth between us, as we were saying goodnight on Mrs. Moon's front porch. When she turned out the light it was time for Ellie to come in. We kissed goodnight and my hands stayed as warm as my heart while I drove ten miles to my home in Oronogo, Missouri.

Over the past fifty years I have bought Ellie beautiful coats and mink jackets, but none could ever take the place of that little tan coat this beautiful sixteen-year-old girl wore that night. One can't believe that so long ago would just seem like yesterday, but love is like that, don'tcha know.

Now, in my senior years, sometimes I look back at my life and I think what beautiful things I would have missed if the three years of war had taken me away forever. The urge is so strong to look up to heaven with outstretched arms and say, "Thank you, Sweet Jesus, for the good times."

By now I have written thousands of words from precious memories and dried millions of happy tears as my mind showed my eyes the image of the beautiful face of the lady that God gave to me. I can almost hear her laughter and feel the warmth of her embrace and tender kiss.

The first and only little spat Ellie and I ever had was when she was a junior in high school. We hadn't seen each other for about two weeks when I went to see her again. Mrs. Moon said it was Ellie's Drum Corps practice night at the gym. She also said it was nice to see me again and that her daughter had missed me. Wasn't that a nice thing for a mother to say? It made me love her even more.

Off to the school gym I went, and as I opened the door to go in, Ellie was pushing the door to go out. When she saw me her scream almost burst my eardrums. Somehow, in all the excitement, the gym door got shut between us. But not for long.

Ellie came bounding out, and as we embraced we told each other we were sorry; for what I don't think we really knew. Forever after, when we heard Jim Reeves or Patsy Kline sing "I Fall to Pieces," it reminded us of that night. Of course, we always sang along and felt the joy that our eyes would tell each other. Needless to say, our dating was back on track for this happy couple on a cold December night.

Speaking of December, Ellie loved Christmas and had her own way of saving up for it. Every month she would stuff folding money into a hobbyhorse that occupied a space in her Christmas collection. Among other sweet things, Ellie became my barber after a haircut I received in Corpus Christi (it was more like a boot camp shearing than a haircut). Of course, I would always tip her well, and that money helped to fill the Christmas bank every month.

I surely must insert here a story about the extent of Ellie's love for me. Around March 1, 1993, when Ellie was so very ill, she kept telling me I needed a haircut. My reply was: "I'll go tomorrow, maybe."

Well, tomorrow never came, as I didn't want to leave Ellie, even with our chliren. I was amazed when a day or two had passed and my girl confronted me again about my hair. She asked me to take her to the bathroom, so I did. To my surprise, she had gotten up by herself and gathered the hair-cutting tools. When I opened the door, there she stood, holding onto the lavatory, tools in hand.

I said, "Ellie, what are you doing?"

She replied, "The shop is open."

Those words just cut my heart in half. They were the same words she had used over the years.

I asked, "Honey, how are you going to do this?"

"I'll show you," she replied.

I helped her to bed and she had me set her on the edge, propped with pillows, and I knelt on the floor. She cut my hair for about twenty or thirty minutes and I could have cared less if she had cut off all of it. I could see the pleasure my girl had in making me the prince she thought I was.

When Christmas shopping time came, my lady always had five to eight hundred dollars for family gifts, and also something extra for the needy. This showed her inner self to be as lovely and beautiful as God had made her outward appearance. Being ever mindful of the needs of others was one of her joys.

Just like her mother, Grandma Lilly, Ellie could not pass the bell ringer and kettle without putting in a contribution. Ellie loved the words penned by Helen Steiner Rice: "Father, I am well aware I can't make it on my own; So take my hand and hold it tight for I can't walk alone. Dear God, as you take our hands and hold them tight, May we realize anew how much we depend on you for guidance and protection. Through our spiritual leadership, we pray for the power to reach out and help others in distress. Amen."

Isn't that precious? It's a lesson for all. Love is like that, don'tcha know!

Well, we would count the savings and plan our shopping till we had our strategy. Excitement would build until we hit the crowds. It was so enjoyable to see the happiness on Ellie's face. That was enough of a Christmas gift for me.

I was good at Christmas wrapping, so it became my fun job.

6

Ellie and I never lost our zest for life even through our fifties, sixties, and seventies. When we remodeled our home or did other things of that nature, she would always remark, "We act like we're going to live forever." We were always too busy with life to think otherwise. Even as senior citizens, we would go trout fishing on opening day at Roaring River State Park in Cassville, Missouri. Some early March mornings would be so cold, ice would freeze on our fishing lines.

One time, being a really good fisherperson, on her second or third cast Ellie caught a nice trout, which I helped her put on her stringer. Later, as we prepared to move to another location, I asked Ellie where the fish was. As I looked around, I saw a lady with a red ballcap carrying it. I asked Ellie if it was hers.

She dropped her rod and reel and confronted the woman. On her return, I asked, "How did you do that so quickly?"

"I told her my uncle Elmer Smith was the sheriff of Cassville," she replied. He really was the Barry County deputy sheriff.

Later, as I prepared to clean the fish, I noticed a tag on the stringer that said: "Ruby Pittman." I had to laugh out loud. I guess those two facts would get anyone's fish back to the rightful owner.

As one can see, we never experienced "cabin fever," as it's called. Once a day, no matter how cold, we would get out of the house if only to go to the mall or walk a couple of miles. This was always nicer than it sounds, because often we saw old friends and, after completing our walk, we would all meet for coffee and have an enjoyable visit.

We also kept our birdfeeders filled so our feathered friends kept flying past our windows. The feeders were our forecaster, because the nearer spring came, the more we noticed different kinds of birds feeding on the seed, which meant they thought winter was coming to an end for this season. These birds remind me of when our first son, Don, was born. We lived in an upstairs apartment in Pueblo, Colorado, and Ellie always fed the birds bread crumbs on the windowsill.

Her sister Mae came to be with us when our son was born. One day Ellie and Mae were watching the birds from the kitchen table over a nice cup of tea when Ellie said, "That little bird looking in the window doesn't have any eyes."

Well, I thought Mae would die laughing. She jested with Ellie for days to come about the "blind bird." Ellie was so blessed with really sweet sisters and brothers.

Every time we got together it was fun times. Later, in the summer, we went to Idaho Springs and Mae accompanied us to Central City, Colorado. We had fun all day long just seeing the sights and enjoying the Western music clubs. When evening came, Mae baby-sat and Ellie and I dressed to the nines for dinner and an evening at the opera. This was really special for two small-town kids like us.

While walking to the car after the opera, Ellie said, "C.E., I love you for our life. Joy always seems to follow after us. Do you think God tells joy to always be around?"

"I'm sure He does," I replied.

She could always make something light up inside of me, and down through the years this light always seemed to get brighter. How sweet it was for God to give us each other.

As we reminisce of more recent years, I remember when the KC Royals were destined to play in the World Series Baseball Classic. We had enjoyed the games all summer long. As time drew close for the fall classic, I applied to Royals Stadium for World Series tickets. As soon as they arrived, which really startled me, I asked Ellie if she would like to go to KC for a World Series game.

She quickly replied, "Please don't joke about this."

78

I asked her to play the kid's game of "shut your eyes and hold out your hands" and gave her the tickets. My, my, you'll never see more jubilation than she displayed. She threw her arms around my neck as we jumped around and around like two nuts, singing, "World Series, here we come," over and over.

While having refreshments at the game, she looked over at me and said, "You always fascinate me by always doing happy things for us."

I swiftly replied, "No, *we* do things together that make the happy times. It's best we never forget that and always be grateful to God."

It was too bad we lost the game, as our pitcher only gave up two hits but lost 1–0. However, our team did win the series. Great memories.

In the song that Barbra Streisand sings called "Memories," life is full of these wonderful times together. Aren't all happy times that way? They are so easy to remember with love.

It seemed our Heavenly Maker planned our life like a road map. He would point out the roads He wanted us to travel. He would make a path He desired us to walk upon. If we followed these instructions, how could our life be other than joyous and happy?

Ellie was always so grateful for her blessings. Every time we came home at 1:00 A.M. from the KC baseball games, she would say, "Thank you, Sweet Jesus, for a safe trip home from a lovely day at the park."

We both believed Jesus was a very influential part of our life, and this created the truest kind of love between us. I have conveyed this thought to you on several occasions. You know God has a very large book and a golden pen in hand. When special people, like you, do nice things, He writes your name in the book for blessings untold!

Ellie had two or three little prayer books that she read daily. Today one such book was marked October 3rd. It explains our relationship with God. We know God's gifts to us always supersede our needs. Sometimes we take all the wonderful gifts for granted and that's cause to stop and adjust our thinking into thankfulness. Isn't God wonderful?

We hadn't lived in our home on Lincoln Street very long when, one winter afternoon, Ellie yelled from the bedroom, "The house is on fire!" I thought she meant ours, but as I dashed to the bedroom I could see it was our neighbor's house. The flames and smoke were belching from a basement door. I told Ellie to call the fire department and ran to the burning house to see if anyone was inside.

The young couple who lived there had enjoyed the birth of twin boys. Thank goodness they were all safe and the fire was extinguished shortly. However, there had been major damage.

As I returned home, here came my sweet lady and she put her arms around my neck and said, "C.E., don't you think the neighborhood will want to help this young couple?"

"Certainly," was my answer.

The cold winter day, with ice- and snow-covered ground and streets, was no match for the love God put into our hearts. By day's end we presented the couple with $200 cash from these lovely neighbors who lived around us. Ellie made a list of all names and addresses and presented it to the young couple along with the cash. After three or four months of repairing their nice home, twins and parents moved back. Not long after, a thank-you card was sent to all givers, those you could say were Good Samaritans. It was just people helping people.

Four years later, this same kindness lived in the hearts of all of us, not just on our tongues. We all enjoyed visiting over the garden gate or sharing a patio cookout. These pleasures are life-warming and come so close to "love thy neighbor as thy self." Close? Only God would know that.

When Ellie and I purchased our lovely old home, we didn't know our neighbor across the street had grown up two houses from our country place. Our neighbor in the first house north of us worked at Sperry Vickers the same time I did. The house next to that belonged to a man who was our rural mail carrier at the country place. It just seems this home was hand-picked for us. Being surrounded by these lovely people made our new life on Lincoln Street in the city so happy.

Over our back fence lived the twin boys and their mother, H.J. Mitch and Russ were four years old now. These three have surely been a blessing to me. They brought sunshine on the most cloudy days. Thank you, guys.

Life moved swiftly and added to the years. Ellie and I awoke one morning and found our golden wedding anniversary (June 14, 1991) was almost here. Ellie gave me a beautiful Elgin watch with a single diamond on its face. I, in return, gave her a single solitaire diamond love ring. In the tender moments that followed, we nurtured these words: "One diamond, one life, one love forever. Thank you, Sweet Jesus."

Our children wanted to have an open house for us, but we had already planned to go to Idaho Springs and Pueblo, where we were first joined together by God. As we drove by the old neighborhoods where we had begun our life together, Ellie said, "Stop. Look up there. See our icebox?"

It was in a north window with a ledge, and we had kept eggs, milk, and butter there. That apartment was the scene of our first Christmas, and she remembered our tree had no lights, just popcorn and cranberry strings. There had been one present under the tree, for luck. However, the whole two rooms were full of Christmas because Jesus visited there with us.

Most all the old neighbors were gone to heaven by now, but we remembered the poor times they had turned into good times. With thankful hearts, we remembered them all, how they touched our lives in such a beautiful way.

Before ending this happy day, we drove up to Idaho Springs, forty miles west of Denver, where we had spent many days with our family, who were all gone to heaven also. We drove by the mountain stream past Ellie's brother Bill's home of forty-five years or so, before his passing. We found the very large mountain stone by the stream where we had picnicked with our children many times. It was where Ellie caught her first trout.

I opened a bottle of spirits, and we exchanged gifts. As the light mountain air blew Ellie's beautiful hair across her pretty face and our lips met so tenderly, we didn't even need to say the words, because the bubbling mountain brook water seemed to say them for us. "I will love you forever and ever," and the words echoed up the canyon to Mount Chief and returned to us in the murmur of whispering pines.

We drove back down to the city, which had changed a lot over the years, from a gold mining town to a tourist town. We had our fiftieth wedding anniversary dinner at the City Cafe. It wouldn't seem much to most people, but Ellie and I had had all the fancy things many times before. Giving her a single red rose from a street vendor as we were walking down the street, hand in hand, lit up her eyes as if to say, "C.E., with you I would do it all over again." Thank you, Sweet Jesus.

The next morning found us heading down the mountain to Denver. Before leaving the city we went to Forest Lawn Cemetery to pay our respects to brother Bill, his wife, Helen, and sister Mae. We just couldn't keep from saying, "Thank God for these lovely people and the good times we had together."

Mae and her husband, Ray, loved to hear Ellie and me sing "For the Good Times," which Ray Price made so popular. They would always applaud and say, "Guys, you get better every time." Of course, we just ate up that sweet talk.

Some family members were so envious of Ellie and me, our home, and our friends. They would so often ask, "How in the world do you guys stay so happy and loving to each other?"

"No bad words and always loving one another," we would always reply. "Love is like that, don'tcha know."

In our realm of family and friends there were heartaches, divorces, and hurts that were so sad. There isn't anything worse

C.E. and Ellie, fiftieth wedding anniversary, 1991. Ellie is seventy, and the author is seventy-two. "How sweet God was to us!"

than a wasted life. Not understanding all the grief, Ellie and I would just pour our hearts out to them and pray to God for guidance and mercy.

As we left Denver, on I-70 East to Joplin, Ellie said, "C.E., do you remember the old song about making a home out in the west?" So we hummed along and put words together before we got to Joplin. It went kind of like this: "Somewhere in the west we'll build our little nest and let the rest of the world go by."

How prettily she could harmonize with me. As we passed through the north edge of Wichita, Kansas, the singing and goofing off had to stop, as we were in the middle of a thunderstorm, tornadoes and all. They followed us to Fort Scott, Kansas, about sixty miles north of Joplin and our home.

As always, in the darkness God just sat along beside us and assured us of a safe trip home. Ellie and I were in our seventies by this time, but from daylight to almost midnight we covered 900 miles. I insert this information to magnify God's love for us. Eternal God, I bless Thee that the light of Thy morning is a fitting symbol to the continual freshness of Thy Grace. I pray that the light of Thy Favor may now rise upon our souls and we may know that we began the day in the will of our Lord. Let our souls awake and sing for this new day allotted us. Hallelujah! Amen.

To give praise and thanksgiving for all of life's blessings always seems to lighten the load of any troubles or adversities. Ellie would often say, "Be thankful for all blessings, large or small." Then she quickly added: "Strike out the last three words, because all blessings are the same size." Isn't that cute? Of course, I think she was cute even when she was brushing her teeth. I'm sure someone, at this point, is saying, "Isn't that disgusting?" But, love is like that, don'tcha know. Or do you?

I know of nothing in the world as sweet as someone you love so dearly saying back to you, "I love you, too, sweetheart." Precious words, precious memories. Oh, how they linger.

It's ironic that today (November 4), Ellie's little prayer book,

Daily Altar, emphasizes my words a few paragraphs ago: "Gracious God, I look to Thee for light and strength. Will Thou let Thy lamp shine upon the appointed road. At the beginning of the road let me find the needed power. Let me walk on the appointed path with a brave and singing heart."

This prayer seemed to be about how we believed God drew a map of the road he wanted us to drive upon and made the paths for us to walk upon from the beginning of our lives together. What joy comes from the throne of God, if only we listen and obey and be ever prayerful every day. If the foregoing testimony has touched the heart of just one couple's life together, then writing until wee morning hours has accomplished a blessing. Thank you, Sweet Jesus.

Isn't it strange that even after enjoying a trip or vacation it's always so nice to get back home? While driving down I-70 to Joplin from Denver, Ellie and I were already planning our next few months. You guessed it. Our houseboat and fishing was the topic.

On our first day of fishing, Ellie caught a really nice black bass and as I tried to net it for her, it went right through the net into the boat. All the time, Ellie was yelling, "Oh no, oh no!" I pounced on the flopping lunker, trying my best to pin it to the bottom of the boat, and was finally successful. However, my hands and elbows took a beating and blood was running down my arms from scratches.

Ellie said, "C.E., you were a tiger cat after that fish."

"I value my life, so I kept him in the boat," I replied.

She just smiled and kissed my hurts away.

Being tired after our trip and fighting that bass, we returned and I made a nice pot of coffee. As the dawn arrived, Ellie was looking out the west window to where, to her amusement, a mama deer and her fawn were standing in the road by our station wagon. The fawn was nursing. Only a couple of weeks before that we had spotted about two dozen wild turkeys in this park. Nature was all around us, it seemed.

When the ten acres was plowed for soybean planting, we always went arrowhead hunting. We were told by old-timers that this had been an early Indian camp. No one could deny that, as we found many arrowheads and tomahawk heads as well. This plot of land was just across the road from where Ellie had seen the deer.

These July and August days were hot, so Ellie and I would go swimming several times a day. Most everyone who had houseboats worked in the daytime hours, and the water was left just for me and my girl.

Our friends and relatives had often asked, "Don't you get bored or lonesome being alone?" I guess they just didn't know my lady and me. We never had time to get lonely. We just enjoyed the precious gift of each other. We had no room for loneliness. We only had time to sing what was in our hearts and dance with happy feet.

Speaking of feet, I recall the summer of railroad gang work. Ellie, with her sister and her husband, came by to see me on their vacation to Idaho Springs. It was on a Sunday, and they took me with them to brother Bill's place. I only had one pair of shoes, and one of them had a large hole in the sole. I got so embarrassed when I thought they could see it that Ellie and I walked behind them.

As we went to a matinee dance in Denver, and I danced Ellie into a far corner, away from her relatives. I was so happy to see Ellie I would have gone with no shoes at all.

Ellie and I were having a Coke at a round table where brother Bill, his wife, Helen, and Chloe and her husband, E.J., sat between dances. Someone told a joke that was so funny we all clapped our hands. I laughed so hard I hit the table with the heel of my closed fist so solidly that it broke the stem of the wineglass Chloe was sipping from. I was terrified of the mess, but everyone assured me it must have been a faulty glass.

Bill was a seasoned fighter and he said, "This kid's so strong from manhandling those jackhammer-type tools that his solid blow did the damage." His next remark was: "I'm going to train you to take my place as the toughest mountain man in these hills."

To my dismay, he stood up and challenged the crowd, saying, "Me and the kid are the best guys in here." Thank goodness there were no takers.

I don't recall how many times, over the years, this subject was brought up. But we all blamed Ellie's sister for breaking her wineglass and almost causing a patrons' riot—all in fun, of course.

Chloe's husband was superintendent of mail for the Postal Service, which was a good job in 1939. He always drove a new car and wore fancy suits. He never thought I should marry Ellie because I wasn't able to give her the kind of life he thought she should have.

This kind of talk was directed to me, all of a sudden, at one of the Sunday matinee dances. Bill said to him, "You have harassed this young man long enough, E.J. Do you understand what I'm saying?"

E.J. was much older than the rest of us, and a wise man to discontinue that kind of talk, for which I was grateful. Nat King Cole's song "Too Young," seems to tell our story with some of Ellie's relatives. But Ellie and I knew that the kind of love God put into our hearts would last forever, and it surely will. True love never dies, don'tcha know?

So we were never too young to know that the loving moments would just keep coming, day after day and night after night.

No one knew, at this time, that youthfulness would never leave us as the years passed. Ellie and I didn't even know how we locked up this youthfulness inside our minds hearts, souls, and bodies. In looking back, our only answer was: "God must have sent angels to do that job."

Ellie, so young and beautiful, was patient with my situation. I was helping my mother, financially, to raise my brother and sisters. Today's young people are influenced so much by peer pressure. Just think how much peer pressure this beautiful eighteen-year-old young lady must have endured. My absence, being 800 miles away, was no help to her. However, you see this is where

God was present in her heart. He just kept us for each other. Is His Spirit strong or what!!

Well, fifty-three years of almost perfect marriage, I'm sure you'll agree, is the appropriate answer.

May I insert here that Ellie and I did not profess to be perfect in any manner? Every human being has his or her faults, which I'm sure God thinks are way too many. However, I do know this for a fact: when we ask His forgiveness, He is ready and willing to forgive. Glory, glory. Amen.

Ellie and I had communion every Sunday. When I laid all my sins before Him in earnest, I walked away with the best feeling a human being can have. As Ellie always said: "Thank you, Sweet Jesus."

7

Getting back to more recent times, I had just found out that one of our dearest friends had cancer of the lungs. Ellie and I were so saddened. We stayed by the family and supported them any way we could. Nadene suffered so much, through two operations and pain on top of pain, until the Lord took her away.

As if that weren't enough, our good friends W. J. and Lois Riley, in Pittsburg, Kansas, were going through the same heartaches. W. J. was operated on for prostate cancer, which prolonged his life for two or three years. You can see how devastating all this was.

We just tried our best to be a blessing to this lovely family who had been friends for over thirty years. It seems as though the words that come from one's mouth, at time like this, are so hollow and shallow. When one gets past seventy, these unhappy events come so swiftly, one after another.

You may think that dealing with tragedy so often would make it a little easier, but it seems they all hurt their own special hurts. So we are compelled to deal with them one at a time and turn to God for blessing and comfort. He tells us He is the way, the truth, and the life. What would we ever do without Him? He always comes to our rescue.

Like the last winter Ellie and I spent in Corpus Christi. We were on our way to Padre Island one day in January 1991. We noticed a new housing development had started around an area called Turtle Cove, and we went to see this beautiful setting. As the houses began to take shape, one could see what they would look like on completion. We just couldn't stop visiting one beautiful place and, after two or three weeks, we made up our minds that it would be good for us to purchase this home and live the rest of our lives in this cozy, warm climate.

We contacted the realty company and made an appointment. You know how realtors are; they always say: "We have several prospects, so don't be late."

Well, lo and behold, the next day we sat in the realtor's lobby and a couple came out of the office. After they left, the realtor asked us in. He informed us that the couple had purchased the only house out there that interested us.

Ellie and I were so disappointed at the time. She always had a sensible explanation, though, for things like this. She said, "It just wasn't meant for us to move."

A few years later, we could see why God took control of the situation. This setback was no hurdle for my lady and me, as we recouped and enjoyed what was to be our last winter together on the sandy beaches where we had had so much fun over the years. The beautiful surroundings just seemed to make love grow!

I believe love grows best in a field of happy people, and most certainly in the fertile lives of faithful couples. God will cultivate and rain upon the seed of love we plant.

The past winters in Texas had taught us the craft of seashells. I don't think any winter ever passed that Ellie and I didn't send little things we made from shells to our many friends and family, things like night-lights and magnet animals for note holders on the fridge. We have a very large mirror hanging on the wall of our stairway landing. Its frame is made of beautiful shells gathered from all over the South Pacific during World War II and our Texas visits.

The following article is in most shell shops, and Ellie found several of the skeletons that it tells about. She dried them in the sun after bleaching them.

It's an interesting story to warm the heart.

It's called the legend of the Crucifix Fish. After the bleached bones are dry, one can shake it and hear a sound like rolling dice, which was done for Christ's robes. This catfish-type fish displays a Roman-looking shield on its back and the front shows a slit-type opening that is said to resemble the sword wound in the side of Jesus.

Ellie and I always thought it was good luck to find these bones because the fish, I'm told, comes to Corpus Christi Bay (in Texas) at Eastertime. We were always back home in Joplin, MO, at the holiday season.

Over the years (about fifteen) we'd take a dozen or so home to give to family and friends. I just loved to hear Ellie explain this cute story to the recipient of the gift. They always seemed to be awed by it.

The story relates that those who shake the bones will be heavenly blessed and Ellie would always say, "I'm going to receive a blessing because I always shake them before giving them away." This action was done to assure that the dice sound was working.

Ellie and I were always blessed with health. However, our 1989 winter trip to Texas would not attest to that statement.

While driving on I-35, just past Dallas, Ellie said, "I feel kind of woozy." She was very quiet the rest of the way to Corpus Christi.

After unloading our winter baggage, she lay on the bed and complained of feeling faint. Our landlord's daughter was a nurse who lived a few doors from us. I called and asked if she could see my wife. Well, it didn't take long for her to see that Ellie was sick.

She called the hospital and Ellie and I were on our way. You know how they do, question after question and then tests. They admitted her on the spot and, as the night progressed, Ellie almost went into shock.

The capable nurses called the doctor who had admitted Ellie. He arrived a short time later and ordered transfusions and blankets, which began to subdue her symptoms. When all the tests were complete, we found out my lady had a bad bleeding ulcer and the doctor implied we were lucky to get to the hospital when we did or the ulcer could have been life-threatening.

By now I'm sure you know what was in my heart, and it wasn't luck. God continued His blessing on my darling. And tender care from me every day and night accelerated her recovery.

In the fifteen winters spent in Texas, the only other illness we contracted was the flu. I'm sorry to say, but so many people at our church were infected that I think that is where we got it. Our condo was about ten miles from our doctor's office, where I had to drive for prescriptions. Of course, visiting the pharmacy was also killing me. The medications didn't take away the symptoms for two or three days, and we were still so sick.

It was the last of February and our lease was up in the middle of March, so Ellie and I decided to go home early. Boy, was that some trip. We hadn't eaten for two days and were only able to drink a small amount of water at a time. Almost nine hundred miles staring us in the face wasn't too great. Ellie and I shared a McDonald's strawberry shake in almost every town until we got home. This time, it really was great to be home.

I think these are the only two times in twenty years that Ellie and I were sick, even counting winter colds. You can imagine how difficult it was for us to cope with not feeling up to par. Ellie had found a large buff-colored polar bear for her collection and, to cheer us up, put him in the front seat with a seat belt and all. She talked to him like a person, things like what he would like for lunch, etc.

As we left I-35 at Gainesville and took Highway 82 to Sherman, we were stopped by a police traffic check. After the routine questions, the officer looked over at Ellie's bear, which she had already named Buffer because of his color, and said, "I see your pet is buckled up, too. Good work, folks. Have a safe trip home."

We felt much better because of the laughter that ensued. By the time we got to Oklahoma, we were feeling better, and we ate a light dinner at McAllister, then decided to drive on home to Joplin.

On our arrival, we could see what was left of a winter snow, so we just put the car in the garage and left the unloading until morning. Ellie fixed us a cup of chicken soup, and we went to bed for a good night's sleep.

Even as bad as we felt, it didn't keep my darling from saying her usual prayer as soon as we drove up the driveway. Her sweet voice, as always, uttered, "Thank you, Sweet Jesus, for a lovely winter and a safe trip home."

I awoke in the morning and opened my eyes to see Ellie looking lovingly into my face. She put her soft, beautiful hand on my cheek and said, "C.E., aren't you ever going to grow old?"

"Why?" I asked.

"Because driving like you did yesterday is a job for a well young man, and you did it even being sick."

My reply was: "Sweetheart, you wouldn't love me if I was old, so I'm staying just like I am. I love you for all day, and now I'm out of here to make you breakfast in bed."

Boy, did that put sparkles in my girl's eyes. The hugs that came later were tender and loving as only my girl could do. While I was fixing poached eggs, bacon, waffles, fresh fruit, and coffee, Ellie fixed her beautiful hair, put on fresh makeup, Chanel #5 cologne, and dressed in her new robe she'd gotten for Christmas. Even in her seventies, she was as beautiful as I can ever remember.

When I came through the dining room with her breakfast tray, I took an artificial rose bud from a flower arrangement on the table and placed it on her napkin. Well, that caused a little tear of happiness. The sweet words from her pretty lips were as if all the love God had put in her heart had spilled over. Only He could know how very much I loved this lady. I can't help from saying she was my best friend, my lady, my love, my wife, my life.

My desire was to always see her happy. I loved to see her smile and hear her laugh. Her beautiful eyes always gave away her deepest feeling; her sweetness always filled the room with the most fragrant happiness.

We were all set for the end of a cold winter, as we had come back early, but it didn't materialize. We had a few nippy days and nights, but spring was on its way. Our red and white dogwoods, as well as our redbud trees, had sprouted buds. Ellie had planted crocus before going to Texas, but as we watched them pop through the ground we knew the package had been mismarked. The bulbs turned out to be English iris with blooms of blue, white, and purple that resembled tiny orchids. The blooms reminded us of picking the baby orchids that grew wild along the roads of Hawaii.

Flowers are like love songs; they belong to a beautiful lady. The gent that remembers to bring her candy and flowers on days other than a birthday or wedding anniversary will surely become her prince of love. Love is like that, don'tcha know.

How wonderful it is, for the giver, to see the light of love shining in the face of the one you just made so happy. I dare to say there is no better way to chase away the clouds of gloom than by expressing your admiration for the precious person in your life. I assure you this act of love is never forgotten, because she will tuck it away in the shadows of her mind. When she is alone with her thoughts, many times the lovely feeling comes back to her. I could always tell when this had happened by the way she greeted me after a long day at work.

There is no greater thrill than when these feelings are transferred from one heart to another. No matter if you are sixteen or seventy years old, that's the way true love works. You must always give thanks to the One you talk to from your pillow every night for this blessing. A thank-you and Amen.

It is hard to understand how these little acts of love can carry so much more importance than a fourteen-karat gold watch or a fur jacket, which seems to get lost in the course of time. They just don't have the place in the shadows of her mind. Flowers and candy are the true symbols of love, I guess.

Precious words, directed to one another, make a threesome with candy and flowers. Jean Kirkpatrick said it well, stating that when mean words are used, they hurt and become a common thought.

However, this logic can be reversed also. True and honest words like *sweetheart, honey,* and *darling* can ultimately become what we think of each other, and that matters, too. Precious words, precious memories, oh how they linger.

It was times like these, when the room was filled with enchantment as we sat on floor pillows by the fire, munching on popcorn, reading good books, or just holding hands while listening to the music of our favorite tapes, this was when the good times of the past and present came from out of the shadows of our minds and flickered before our faces as the flames flickered above the burning logs while the smoke vanished up the chimney forever. Memories always return another day and another time to smooth away the lonely tears, some of them sad, but for the most part happy tears.

Many times, Ellie and I would just cover up with a heavy afghan, turn the lights off, and go to sleep on the floor, holding hands as usual. We'd awake in the early morning hours to find the cheery fire had burned to ashes, like memories that had vanished in our sleep.

However, the romance in our life never vanished or faded. The magic feeling of love that God had placed in us must have been sealed by His hand. Awake or asleep, we were always in love. To awaken to the sight of her pretty face was a lifetime of joy to me.

Soon it was early April and the dogwoods were just beautiful in full bloom. It was time to make our houseboat, on Spring River, ready for summer fun. It seemed as though keeping our summer place safe and in good shape was taking more time each year. The fall of 1992, September to be exact, we experienced one of the worst floods ever. The water was thirty feet above the road where Ellie had seen the mama deer and her fawn. The flood washed away every houseboat from space 1 to space 20, except for space 5 and our space 20. This meant eighteen houseboats had washed away between the entrance gate and our place.

The loss was mostly caused by neglect. The holding cables, pipes, and floating devices had to be checked and repaired every summer. However, most owners were too busy and that was their downfall.

One day, during upkeep, Ellie said, "C.E., we are getting too old for this kind of work every year. Do you think we should sell our place and find something different to do in the summer?"

Well, that just about knocked my socks off. Later in the day, we stopped to rest. I got us cold drinks and put the lawn chairs on our front deck so Ellie and I could pursue her question. My mind traveled back to Idaho Springs and the year her brother Bill passed away. He didn't leave a will, so the estate was divided among the nearest kin; Ellie's sisters and brother George. That was the year 1967, and real estate wasn't too easy to sell. Brother Bill and Helen had fixed up their mountain home over the years and kept it in good repair. It had three bedrooms, a very large living room and a beautiful fireplace sitting on five acres with a mountain stream running across one corner. It was a beautiful setting with blue spruce trees and all.

They couldn't get a buyer at $50,000 and asked everyone involved to OK a price reduction to $40,000. At the time, Ellie and I talked about paying the price and keeping it for a summer vacation place. Now, as you can imagine, as this idea was talked about, there was some static. So, after all these years being so close and happy, Ellie and I dropped the subject right away.

Today, however, as we discussed selling our houseboat, I asked if buying a summer place in Idaho Springs still sounded like a good idea. My beautiful girl came over and sat on my lap, put her arms around my neck, and whispered, "Let's go there on our wedding anniversary and check it out. It's only a month away and we can call the Idaho Springs paper and run ads prior to our arrival."

Now remember, we were past seventy at this time. See what I meant, some pages ago, when I said we did things like we were going to live forever?

We did go on our anniversary, June 14.

Casino gambling, by this time, was in full swing in adjoining counties, and real estate had skyrocketed. Bill and Helen's home and five acres were worth about \$150,000 to \$175,000, so our dream of a summer place vanished.

By now, I'm sure you know, this didn't stop Ellie and me from having an enjoyable summer vacation in the mountains. Ellie got to catch some trout a couple of days before we headed home. Little did we know this would be our last visit to these beautiful mountain parks where love had flourished between us over many, many years.

About halfway to Wichita she said her famous line to me again: "C.E., it just wasn't meant for us to find our summer place here."

We made it back home to Joplin with most of the summer left to enjoy. Boating, fishing, and going to KC for Royals baseball were pleasures hard to resist for Ellie and me. We decided to keep our houseboat and bought a real nice trihull, walk-through windshield Glasstron boat. We were sure this convertible-top beauty would enhance our enjoyment, and for the rest of the summer it surely did.

We were still trying to complete our repairs to the houseboat, and as I leaned over the railing, my brown cowboy hat fell into the water on the upstream side. Our efforts to retrieve it were futile. That evening, while we were eating dinner on the deck, my hat came floating out from under the houseboat where it had stayed all afternoon. It was so weird; it was floating top up, as if someone were wearing it. Ellie and I just laughed as it floated downstream and out of sight.

The next day, at home, my darling came back from shopping and presented me with a new white hat. Now, that was sweet. Don't you agree?

The following morning, while I was mowing the lawn, Ellie called me to the phone. My World War II marine friend was on his way to Joplin and wanted to be sure we would be home for a couple of days as he was leaving from Arizona. Smitty stayed with us a couple of days, and we reminisced about the old war days. His wife had passed away the year before with lung cancer.

It's amazing how emotions are stirred by past experiences.

When Smitty arrived in our driveway, we greeted each other with a friendly hug and teary eyes. My friend Ron Smithiger and I are the only two we know of who still correspond from our old First Marine Division of fifty years ago. Time really does change things and people.

But, as my friend Smitty said: "Some things about World War II you don't forget."

We were very close, almost like brothers. Each had depended on the other to protect his life many times.

For example, ten or twelve years after the war, Ellie, our daughter, Patricia, our son Donald, and I were on our way for a summer vacation at Idaho Springs. We stopped to have breakfast at a roadside restaurant. The place was full, so we waited for a table. I noticed a man, sitting at a table with three or four other men, staring at us.

I asked Ellie if we knew him and her reply was negative.

As we sat down at our table the man got up and came over. He said, "Doc, if you are Pittman, you saved Captain Budge's life at Peleleiu. We were in the First Marines there."

My memory wasn't as sharp as his, because when you patch up so many they all become "Mac," the general name for an enlisted man. However, I didn't let on to him; I just gave him a hug.

He said, "Doc, we owe you guys a lot."

I can see him now, walking back to his table and friends, only to return as they were leaving. He shook hands with all of my family.

Ellie was shook up from all this and didn't eat much of her breakfast. When it was time to hit the road again, after paying for our breakfast and a full tank of gas, we were on our way. Ellie scooted over close to me, in the middle of the front seat, put her arms around my shoulder, laid her pretty head on me, and said, "C.E., why didn't you tell us about this?"

I replied. "There wasn't that much to it, sweetheart."

She squeezed me tight and kissed my cheek as if she understood. That was my girl; she could just read my mind. She knew I didn't want to talk about it, and the way she complied was so precious to me. Love is like that, don'tcha know. You know that only if you have a special lady like my Ellie.

The rest of the day she seemed to want to stay close to me, as if she thought I would leave without her. I guess she was thinking about all those lonely days and nights, month after month, when World War II was in progress. I'm sure in her heart she was thanking Sweet Jesus for these moments we were sharing together right now.

I asked Smitty if he remembered the marine's name. He joking retorted, "Can't say as I do, Doc. However, there were so many unheralded heroes and most of them, like us, wouldn't trade moments like that for all the accommodations the military had to offer."

Smitty slept in one of our upstairs bedrooms at our house, where Ellie had her teddy bear collection. He was intrigued with her little critters. Smitty kidded Ellie by saying, "Did you know they talk all night long?"

When Smitty got to his home, he sent her a furry bear and a wind chime with three ceramic teddy bears that made a musical sound when they clanged together. He was a good friend and made my girl smile.

I felt so sorry for him going home to an empty house. I thought how awful it must be to be left alone after sharing all those years with the one you love. I guess that's why Smitty called so often, wanting us to come to Phoenix for a visit. He even offered to take us to Canada in his motor home on a fishing trip. Ellie and I were seriously considering this offer in the summer months, but it's too cold in Canada in the winter. It seems as though time just ran out for Ellie and me to experience this pleasure.

Smitty left shortly afterward to attend his high school class reunion in Davenport, Iowa. Ellie and I were off to our houseboat and fishing.

8

It was a Friday afternoon, and Ellie took her tape player and tapes out so we could dance on our front deck. Here we were, seventy-two and seventy-five years old and still having dates on Fridays. These times were, as ever, a thrill, to hold my darling and dance away the afternoon. Ellie was still so graceful and beautiful. We never stopped doing the fast dances like the jitterbug and the shag; these kept us young. Of course, the slow dances kept us youthful also.

For many years now, we had told our family and relatives that Fridays were our special days to be alone and do the things that made us happy. But that didn't matter; they just didn't understand that people our age still had the capacity to enjoy dancing and loving and being happy just by being with each other.

Ellie and I were like a special bottle of wine. We were vintage; we were choice human beings and truly an example of God's love. How else could we be so in love even in our older years? It was like unto the dawn of a new day instead of the evening sunset. How truly happy we were, trying our best to walk the paths that God had laid before us.

Well, as this beautiful day had been overcome by darkness, Ellie and I packed up to go home. We were going to a Sunday KC Royals baseball game. We chose to travel the country road home, which paralleled the river for several miles. This night, we turned off the pavement to the gravel road that led us by corn- and soybean fields.

We saw a pair of very shiny eyes ahead, and Ellie said, "Look at those bright eyes."

I slowed the car so as not to excite whatever it was. As we

approached, we could see it was jet black. It turned and jumped the cattle fence and began to run across the field.

I said, "Ellie, you are seeing a panther." I could tell what it was by the way it loped in the moonlight.

For one of the few times in our life, my girl was not 100 percent buying this. Well, to her amazement, our morning *Joplin Globe* newspaper printed an article about a cemetery worker seeing a black panther in the same area a week or so before.

I loved for Ellie to doubt, once in a while, because she would always come to me and say she was sorry. Boy, how she could say she was sorry! It was one of my life's pleasures.

We proceeded home after this thrilling event. Ellie scooted over close to me as the radio played "Smoke Gets in Your Eyes," a tune Ellie and I had danced to many times down through the years. As it ended, she turned off the radio and asked, "C.E., if I ever get sick or they want to operate on me, would you not let them do it?"

This statement, out of the blue, just floored me. I said, "Why do you ask me this now?"

Her reply was that her friend Nadene Webb, who passed away with cancer, always said, "Ellie, you and C.E. dance that song as if you were in the movies. You just know what step he is going to do."

I said, "Ellie, all my life has been lived to please you and to make you happy. How could I stop now?"

The next Saturday morning I was at the Auto-Express getting new V-belts put on Ellie's Olds Eighty-eight. It only had 40,000 miles on the odometer but was eleven years old, and the belts had started to crack and glaze. In all the traveling in our business, over the years, we didn't have any auto trouble because, like with our houseboat, we prided ourselves on preventive maintenance.

Sunday morning arrived and found us on our way to the baseball game. We stopped at the McDonald's in Lamar for a rest and had sausage and biscuits and coffee. I put Ellie back in the car and checked the tires as I always did when we traveled. I got behind the wheel and turned the key, but nothing happened. I checked the battery and it was dead. I thought, *How can that be? It's still under warranty.*

Here it was, Sunday and no place open to fix it. The gas station next door listed names and phone numbers of private businesses that would get it started. The one I called showed up after about an hour. The man checked the alternator and said it wasn't charging the battery. He charged our battery enough, he said, to get us back to Joplin.

I paid him his fee, which was the easy part. Now I had to tell Ellie there would be no ball game today. To my surprise, she said she really didn't feel too hot anyway. I thought she was just being nice to me, as she always was.

We turned the Olds around and headed back to Joplin. We made it without a hitch. On arrival home, I put the battery charger on so we could have power to get our alternator fixed or replaced the next morning.

The first place we took it for repair showed me that a wire was disconnected and that was the problem. I guess the Auto-Express had done that while putting on the new V-belts two days before. The company reimbursed us for the baseball tickets and the service call in Lamar.

When I got home, my girl had fresh coffee ready and buttered breakfast rolls just out of the oven. I said, "Ellie, let me put all this on a tray and we'll go to the patio porch swing and sit in the morning sunshine."

It was a beautiful summer morning with large white, fluffy clouds in a beautiful blue sky, typical of a Missouri summer. I asked Ellie if she was feeling any better than yesterday, and she assured me she was.

We always had physicals and flu shots this time of year, hoping it would keep us well through the winter. Our appointment was for the following week, so I asked Ellie to tell the doctor that she had not been feeling up to par.

September days, down through the years, were always special

to Ellie and me because God had turned our eyes toward each other at 10:00 A.M., September 1, 1937.

Sometimes I look back to my boyhood, when Ezra Kilmer, a twelve-year-old friend, and I lay on top of his brother's haystack, looking up into the darkened sky, counting the brightest stars, and dreaming of what our future was going to be. Ezra dreamed of being a fire chief in California, where he would be moving in about a month. I don't ever remember dreaming about jobs, positions, or lifetime employment. The movies of the silver screen fascinated me with their love stories and "romanticized" me at a young age, which ultimately made me the romantic that I am today. At least, that's what I've been told many times.

I just hope that those of you who know the thrill of a moonlight stroll and holding hands with the one you love or going to sleep at night holding someone's hand and wishing the night would speed away to an early dawn so you can have the joy of each other in a brand-new day and a new kind of love are as thankful as Ellie and I were. I guess God puts these desires on our hearts and leaves it up to us to pursue them. However, I think He must have given Ellie and me a little push to get us started on our way to a love unparalleled in our private realm of relatives and friends or in books and movies. His constant presence in our lives attested to the authenticity of our love for each other.

I would have to be like the Apostle Paul to profess God's part in our lives: "I am not ashamed of the Gospel of Christ, for it is the Power of God unto salvation to every one that believeth, to the Jew first and also the Greek" (Rom. 1:16) and "For there in the righteousness of God revealed from faith to faith, as it is written, the just shall live by faith" (Rom. 1:17).

I guess what I'm trying to say is that Ellie and I always believed our marriage was made in heaven and it was by faith that we professed God's effect on our life together. I say to you that there is no other power in heaven or Earth that could have given Ellie to me. We lived our lives by faith. As my darling would say: "Thank you, Sweet Jesus. Amen."

Getting back to the day in September on the patio porch swing, I had just come back with fresh cups of coffee for Ellie and me. While sipping them with exaggerated noises and teasing one another, we decided to go to an indoor flea market. Ellie was trying to find a miniature china tea set like little girls might get for Christmas. Here again, these little girl things absent from her childhood seemed to give her joy now. Our home attested to that; two pretty china dolls rocking side by side in a little girl's rocking chair in our living room by the fireplace. Precious memories, oh, how they linger.

Ellie always kept little secret things to herself. When we purchased our present home, on Lincoln Street in Joplin, she was forever wanting to go to the furniture stores. I inquired what she wanted to buy, and she replied, "Oh, I just want to look around."

One morning, as we were reading the newspaper, she jumped up and said, "Come on, C.E. Let's go."

"Where?" I asked.

"I'll show you," she said as she dashed into the bathroom to change into street clothes and makeup, which she didn't really need (makeup, that is). She didn't need makeup because her pretty face was like an angel's.

By now I hope you know that there is no greater happiness in the life God gives us than a couple truly in love, guided by His love and mercy.

Well, we went to Ward's Furniture. As she gazed at a Duncan Phyfe hall table with a matching wall mirror I could see the joy in her eyes. She said, "C.E., isn't this beautiful? It even has the drawer like I really wanted." She concluded it was for her special things.

I thought, *No need for my comments, because a lady needs her own little special secret things that are close to her heart.*

She ran her pretty hand over this prize she had found. I paid the salesperson, and he directed me to the shipping department so we could put this purchase in our station wagon. I took Ellie's arm and told her what we must do to get her table home. All the time, she was telling the shipping department employees, "Please, don't scratch my table."

Isn't that just like a lady, nice and neat and unmarred?

As we placed the table in the hallway, she asked me to bring the box that was in her cedar chest.

"Now I want to show you what precious things belong in here," she remarked. "First, shut your eyes and hold out your hand."

I did, and she placed a wedding anniversary card I had sent her from the Pacific during the war (1943). No wonder she wanted something special like this little table we had bought.

"Hold on," she said. "Let's do it again." So I shut my eyes and held out my hand, and in it she placed a little empty Evening in Paris perfume bottle from the first Christmas present I bought her, when she was only fifteen and a sophomore in high school (1937). I don't know how long we stood there, embraced in each other's arms. No words came from our lips as the tears ran down our cheeks. Ellie twisted my hair in her fingers to make a curl on the back of my head.

I gently held her at arm's length, looked into her tear-filled green eyes, and said, "Angel face, you beat all. Where have you had these all these years?"

She still didn't say a word; she just touched her finger to her heart. Now, that really is love, don'tcha know.

When we finally calmed our emotions, I said, "Sweetheart, let's dress up like we used to for a candlelight dinner and an evening of slow dancing."

Boy, what an enjoyable evening with my beautiful lady. She was so tender and refreshing, always so loving and beautiful.

We were in our late sixties at this time, and as I looked at her across the candlelit dinner table, she was as pretty as any time in the years past. I marveled at this and thought, *It's as it should be, because we are God's special people.*

105

When we arrived home, she thanked me for a lovely evening and for her little treasure table. When I talked to God about the joys in life, what else could I say but, "Thank you, Sweet Jesus, for this precious person and the love you cultivate between us?"

Before I shut my eyes to sleep that night, I was also thankful for that little fifty-year-old perfume bottle, which was a symbol of Ellie's true love. What more could my life need?

After this special evening together, we were having our morning coffee. Ellie was busy putting other little memories in her hallway table drawer. She showed me the little "Love is" notepads ("Love is" are sentiments from Kim and Robert's *Real Life Romance*) where she had scribbled: "Love is C.E." At the bottom of the note was printed: "Love is dancing to slow, misty music." Wow!

One Valentine's Day, I had given Ellie a little booklet called *1001 Reasons Why I Love You*. The first line of the first page said: "I love you cuz you say the right things when I need 'em most." The following twenty pages are full of similar love notes.

She handed me a small fifty-page book of poems. Page 6 had a bookmarker for the poem "How Do I Love Thee" by Elizabeth Browning, and Ellie's note at the top of the page indicated it was her favorite. "How do I love thee, let me count the ways. I love thee to the depth and breadth and height my soul can reach . . ."

Ellie had also marked page 49 with the note: "Isn't this beautiful. To my dear and loving husband."

If ever two were one, Then surely we.
If ever man were lov'd by wife then Thee.
If ever wife were happy in a man
Compare with me, ye women, if you can.
I prize thy love, more than whole mines of Gold
Of all the riches that the Earth doth Hold.
My love is such that rivers can not quench
nor ought but love from thee give recompense.
Thy love is such I can no way repay.

Then while we live, in love let's so persevere
That when we live no more, we may live forever.

by Anne Bradstreet

The book jacket cover photo was from Franco Zeffirelli's *Romeo and Juliet* (Paramount Pictures).

Ellie's and my love poems were not expressed by written words upon a page, but carried forever in our hearts so deep that temptations of life could not erase the faithfulness of the love God placed upon us.

Now, I'm sure you can see that all the dreams of the twelve-year-old country boy from the little lead and zinc mining town of Oronogo had reached life's full bloom, like the roses of the morning. My Ellie would say, "C.E., your roses are just beautiful today." Her image is etched in my mind, as she looked out our kitchen window upon our garden of roses, which were no match for her beautiful face framed by the floral color of her morning coat. Yes, I know you want me to say again: "True love is like that, don'tcha know."

Now, let the world see your smile!

For the last few minutes we have journeyed through a garden of love words that can only be spoken of a boy and girl living in this rapturous moment.

As the morning progressed, it was time to ready ourselves for an afternoon doctor's appointment for checkups and flu shots. While I was paying for our office call, Ellie came up to me and said, "C.E., I have an ear infection, which may be the cause of my problems."

She showed me a prescription for antibiotics as we were going to the car, and we picked it up at the pharmacy before going home. As Ellie was opening the bag, she noticed the price of the pills was almost fifty dollars and remarked, "I wonder why the doctor didn't give me the usual Amoxicillin? It's only eight or ten dollars."

Her doctor thought her cough could be attributed to her

infected ear. I said, "Ellie, maybe that's the reason for the new pills."

Ellie had been on this medication for three or four days when she complained of breathing difficulties and swollen ankles. I called the doctor. His nurse said she would give him the information and promised to call me back, which she did. The doctor's reply to our problem was that Ellie's infected ear was most likely the culprit and advised her to see her ear, nose, and throat doctor. As she had been his patient for seven or eight years, it was difficult for me to understand his logic. I think any patient would have been very disappointed with his lack of attention to our problems. It turned out to be very serious.

We went to another doctor and then to a lung specialist. An X ray showed a spot on Ellie's lung. God almighty only knows the torture of the next sixth months as we were told, after a biopsy report, that Ellie had a malignancy in her left lung.

I was so furious about our family doctor for not pursuing Ellie's bad cough a couple of months prior. The doctor who performed the biopsy encouraged us to have other, extensive tests performed to make sure there was no malignancy anywhere else.

It took many sleepless nights before we found out that all other tests were negative, for which I sent praises up to God.

It was a week since we had been given the devastating news, and we took time for Ellie and me to sit down at our houseboat deck, hold hands, and pour our hearts out to one another. You have no idea how much hurt can come from two hearts that were so in love. We were trying to salvage what was left of a dream life that had always been sheltered by God's great mercy and love. We turned to the One we had known and loved from the beginning of our life together and asked Him to direct us and place His bountiful mercy upon us and strengthen us to endure the unknown that lay ahead.

Down through the years, Ellie and our children thought that I could fix most anything. But, as we talked on our houseboat in the early autumn sun that warmed us, we had to admit that this problem was now up to the medical community and God.

It was difficult to understand in 1937, when God first introduced us to each other, how precious this time of year was. Now, when separation was so definite because of this terminal illness, the autumn seemed different. The songs "Falling Leaves" and "September in the Rain" took on a whole new meaning.

Ellie was steadfast in her wishes about no operations, no rest homes, and no life supports. As we sat close to each other, she squeezed my hand and looked into my eyes. Vacant of tears now, she said, "Darling, will you take care of me so I can pass from our home and you up to heaven when the time comes?"

She really didn't need to ask that question, because I don't recall not respecting any of her wishes for all these years. Any request my Ellie ever made was attainable and sensible.

But every day, I tried so hard to pursue the possibility of an operation, reasoning with my girl that time was of the essence. The days of caring for this precious one now seemed so short. The dawn to evening passed so quickly.

It became difficult for Ellie to read her Bible at night, so for the next several months we studied it together and professed Jesus to each other.

One evening, she was looking at the literature from her oncology doctor and said, "C.E., you don't agree with my decision, do you?"

I could only reply, "I can't answer that, sweetheart, because I'm not you. You know, if it were me, what I would do."

She just looked straight into my face for the longest time. It seemed her eyes were searching my mind for some answer. Finally, she said to me, "C.E., do you think our doctor would still give me chemotherapy?"

I just about fainted. I replied, "We sure can find out."

In the morning, we were on our way to take the first treatment at nine o'clock.

In the times that followed, when I helped Ellie to the bathroom, we'd hold each other and pretend we were dancing again. We still tried to be happy even in this most difficult time.

I often saw a searching in her beautiful eyes, as if she were looking at happier times, when we still possessed hopes and dreams and happy tomorrows, times we had thought would last forever. We were always too busy with life and too much in love to ever think we would come to these dark days.

Ellie and our children would always say, "Dad can fix it no matter what." And now I was angry at myself because I couldn't fix this most tragic situation. I found myself asking, *Why were we given such a special life, just to be parted from each other now?*

All the important things of life had lost their savor. The people I love didn't even seem the same. The early morning coffee in sunshine had lost its flavor. At twilight, the rising moon that Ellie and I always found so romantic had lost its magic. Life just seemed to have become unimportant. The value of life, which Ellie and I placed on most everything, had been bent out of synch.

I suppose God will find me somewhere in this dark world and say, "Hey, guy, you are still an important person," and encourage me to finish this manuscript in His and Ellie's honor. With His help, I am sure I will. God's love is like that, don'tcha know.

For weeks before the chemotherapy started, nurses had been coming to see Ellie twice a week. They were so precious and good to my lady. Of course, these visits ended when Ellie decided to take chemo, as these nurses were from Hospice, a beautiful, caring organization for terminal patients.

It was difficult for Ellie to walk, so our children helped us in and out of the car when we went to the doctor's. Ellie needed my help to go to the bathroom or to get in and out of bed.

One morning, as we were getting ready for a doctor's appointment, I helped Ellie to the bathroom to brush her teeth. As I held her up to the lavatory, she passed out in my arms. I picked her up and laid her gently on the bed and called the doctor.

I had propped Ellie's feet up on two pillows, and she came to as I was on the phone by the nightstand. I just hung up the phone and attended to my girl. We got to the doctor's office, and after hearing our report, he put her in the hospital for a week of blood tests and a brain CAT scan, which revealed that she had had a stroke.

I could not go home and leave this most important part of my life, so I stayed every night, and our three children, Patricia, Don, and Roy Mark, came at different times during the day. By now it was becoming difficult for Ellie to eat, so we, along with the nurses, fed her like a baby. We would kid along and sometimes got a smile as our reward.

Ellie's doctor came early in the morning, about 6:00 A.M., for hospital calls. One morning, he and the nurse came to me and said, "Mr. Pittman, we have previously told you that your missus had a few months. But, since all the tests are now in, it may be only days."

The doctor put his hand on my shoulder and asked if he could do anything for me. I replied, "Yes. Make Ellie get up from bed and walk home with me."

The nurse put her arms around me and let her tears fall with mine.

After we got Ellie home, I didn't tell our children what I had been told, in hopes it could save them some grief. That was Ellie's wish when she first knew of her illness, not to tell anyone because of the upcoming holidays. This precious, unselfish person lived out her prayer, which was to be made ever mindful of the needs of others.

I can still hear her sweet voice saying our Thanksgiving dinner Grace: "Thank You, Lord, for another day and for health and family and love and forgiveness, and make us ever mindful of the needs of others."

So very very sweet this was coming from a lovely lady who did not possess health but was thankful for what life she had left. I have never seen a person so brave. Ellie never complained and never said, "Why me?" She only said, when we sat on the bed together, holding each other so closely and talking heart to heart,

111

"C.E., I don't want to leave you and the kids. Who will take care of you? No one knows how but me."

Now, it's memories like that which tear at the heart. The most difficult thing in my life was to watch this once-vibrant, beautiful person dwindle slowly away. Sometimes she would hold up her bare arms and just stare at them as if those once-shapely arms were now dwindling away.

After the Christmas of 1993, we celebrated Ellie's birthday on December 29. I baked a cake with fresh strawberries and invited the children for a birthday lunch. Ellie enjoyed it so much. It was the first time in many weeks that I saw a flicker of joy in her eyes. Oh, how I praised God for that.

When Ellie and I had our fiftieth wedding anniversary pictures made, we had received one that was fourteen inches by sixteen inches, which I had framed in an oval wooden frame for Ellie's birthday. After her birthday lunch, I presented her with the package.

As she opened it, her beautiful green eyes went wide with amusement. It was so beautifully done. Ellie just held it close and caressed it with her long, pretty fingers as if to show me her approval and pleasure. I kissed her and wished her "Happy Birthday" as we sang the birthday song. God had blessed her with seventy-two years today, a few more days than her doctor had thought.

Cooking for Ellie was not easy for me, because she had been such a good cook. This didn't stop me from baking her a double-layer birthday cake with whipped topping and strawberries. it wasn't too bad, as she ate every crumb. That gave me courage to keep trying.

Late every spring, Ellie and I had driven about twelve miles to pick blueberries. We always got about three gallons to freeze and give to friends and family. I rummaged through Ellie's recipes and found how to make a blueberry pie, lattice-top crust and all. I was so proud to show it to Ellie before it was sliced into pieces. We sure had fun laughing about it, and it didn't taste bad either.

The blueberry patch where we had picked berries was so neat; the grass was mowed between the rows. On our last picking, Ellie had slipped into a hole that was hidden by the mown grass and fallen, spilling her bucket of berries. She cried, because of embarrassment mostly, but we just salvaged what we could and finished picking until her bucket was full again.

I kidded her that this pie I had just baked was made from her spilled berries. As we were eating, I would make believe I had found a blade of grass in my piece. That caused a little laughter also.

Even in these darker days, God was still helping us to have what little joy was left. Even when I helped Ellie to the bathroom, holding her hands, we made believe we were dancing, which had been a lifelong joy for my girl and me. When she was ready to go back to bed, she would say, "C.E., dance me back." That I would do, with our arms around each other. I would kiss her as I laid her gently down.

She had always smelled so sweet and good all her life, so we changed her PJs every morning so Ellie would feel fresh and clean after I gave her a daily bath. I found out in a hurry I should wash her PJs every day and not let them stack up. I learned to comb my pretty lady's hair in an upsweep and I used her pearl comb to keep it in place. We always put on her favorite jewelry, pearls, earrings, and rings. She was always ready for Sister Careen, hospice nurse, or friends.

When Ellie was in the hospital, all the nurses marveled at how prettily I could fix her hair. Of course, they were being nice, but I liked the kind words. It always caused a cute little smile from my darling.

You remember that Ellie liked to watch the birds from our breakfast table, so I fixed a feeder just outside her room window. What a joy this small act brought her.

I awoke one morning, a few days after fixing the birdfeeder, to a snowfall that had covered the ground. During Ellie's morning trip to the bathroom, I took her by the window to see the redbirds feeding; they were sitting in the snow and pecking up the fallen crumbs. I could tell this was a pretty sight for my girl. She had such a happy expression on her darling face.

January 1994 was almost gone and one of our favorite holidays was approaching: Valentine's Day. Why not our favorite? We were sweethearts that even sweethearts looked up to. Please, I don't mean to sound boastful. Many times our younger relatives and friends would tell us how they admired us and used us as an example. We would always comment, "It's God's work, so please give Him the praise." I could almost always hear Ellie say, under her breath, "Thank you, Sweet Jesus."

I don't think those precious words from her beautiful lips will fade from my memory even in death.

Jeanie, my next-to-the-youngest sister, would write on her greeting cards to Ellie and me: "Thank you for setting an example for us. You are such a very special couple." Ellie would smile that cute smile and say to herself, "Jeanie, you're sweet." Believe it or not, even at this most trying time, I still get a chuckle just writing down these words.

Getting back to Valentine's Day, which brings back such fond memories when we always went to Hawaii for the month of February, because it was set aside for lovers. These were so very, very special moments in our lives. I'm so glad we chose holidays and happy times together in lieu of being monetarily wealthy. The U.S. Mint couldn't house the means to acquire these elegant days and nights of holidays together.

For Valentine's Day, I had sent off for a Valentine picnic wicker chest with truffles, candy, nuts, roses, and sparkling cider. It was so tastefully arranged that I could just imagine Ellie's expression on the day I would give it to her. She enjoyed pretty, unusual things. She also loved surprises.

This didn't stop her from asking me if I had bought her a Valentine! I asked "Why?" and she said, "You know, I always wanted to have the white gold band on my snowflake diamond ring replaced with yellow gold."

I kidded her by asking, "Would that alone make you happy?" The answer was a cute little smile and: "Yes."

The very next day I hurried off to our jeweler friend and accomplished Ellie's request in time for Valentine's Day. Of course, one of our children came to stay with their mother while I was gone. Ellie missed me when I wasn't with her, and as soon as I returned she would always say, "Why were you gone so long?"

I was amazed that she was that alert. One could see her fading day by day now. It was so difficult to get her to eat and drink her vitamins. This demon inside my love was causing her body to repress her desire for food. Every day I tried to fix the special things she always liked, but that didn't help either. She loved malts and shakes, and almost every night she would let me feed her a different flavor, so this helped to nourish her.

Just a few days after Valentine's Day, we reminisced about these love-filled past years. Afterward, Ellie said, "C.E., come sit by me and let's talk about our burial lot." She explained that she didn't want to be buried there anymore. I asked her where she wanted to change to. She named the cemetery where many friends, my brother Howard, and his daughter had been laid to rest. I assured her I would take care of this early tomorrow, which I did.

We had purchased the original plots, next to Grandma Lilly, forty years ago. But since then Joplin had grown, and the North Park Mall was built just across the street. Ellie exclaimed that it would be too noisy. Whatever reason, I didn't care, I just wanted to set her mind at ease. It seemed as thought this last request, from this most precious part of me, calmed all her fears. She began to sleep almost all the time.

I cannot begin to tell you how awfully lonely and sad it was, to be with the one I loved more than life itself, without a smile or words of love, day after day and night after night.

I tried to go to sleep early, because we would awaken many

times in the night. Ellie would always arouse me from sleep by taking her hand away from mine. We had slept holding hands for more years than I can remember. She was taking medication around-the-clock also. I had to give her hypodermic medicine in the stomach four times a day.

February 1994 was soon history, which reminded me that Ellie always fixed a little Irishman's party for me on Saint Pat's Day: corned beef and cabbage with a trimming of a green bow tie and derby hat, make-believe Irish spirits with green straws. This was how we lived every day, just making each other happy with our tiny efforts. Of all the things we gave each other over almost sixty years nothing was a match for giving ourselves in the most sincere and faithful love to each other.

I can see clearly now why God was always in our life, because we three were in love together.

On March 12, Ellie tried to talk to me a little more than usual. This happened when I woke her to give her a drink of water and her medication. She seemed to want to hold onto my hand, which I was always willing to do because that was our symbol of love. Remember our first meeting at the roller rink, when her sister wouldn't let me take her home? I was satisfied to stand with her and hold hands with the most beautiful girl I had ever seen, the one I just knew God would send to me from my childhood wishes. All these years we almost always went to sleep holding hands.

Barbara Mandrell's love song "After All These Years," tells my feelings so well.

When Ellie and I were together 100 percent, not a day went by without planning something for tomorrow. Dreams that kept us so very young even past our seventies—we were still dreamers and lovers. Every day gave us new hope for tomorrow. Hope that our dreams could materialize into reality and they most always did. God loved us, don'tcha see.

After all these years, you wouldn't think I'd cry, but I still love her; after all, you were my life. Now the page upon which I have written these words is wet with tears and attests to my love forever for this God-given gift, my lady, my love, my wife, and my life. Thank you, Sweet Jesus, from me, C.E.

That night Ellie and I were awake together many times. The last time I remember it was 3:30 A.M. and we held hands as we nestled down to get another hour of sleep.

I woke again about 6:30 A.M., and I could feel her once warm and loving hand was cold in final sleep. I couldn't turn loose as I tried to control my emotions. I gently laid her hand upon her breast. . . .

As I write down these memories, now, I think back about Ellie's swollen ankles and feet. The last day we went shopping together, we purchased four or five different kinds of lotions to massage her feet with every night. They seemed to bother her mentally more than anything. Now that her days were being so difficult, her only escape from reality was to sleep. However, caring for Ellie's swollen feet did give us a chance to utter the love words to each other that had been so endearing all our life together.

I had to think how Jesus had disrobed himself when his days were growing slim as well, and with a pail of water and a towel he washed every Apostle's feet and commanded them to do likewise with one another.

Her feet and the loving touch of her hands were always so warm and gentle. My mind just can't comprehend the coldness of the darkness of this dawn. I could see Ellie's feet when she walked her babies to sleep, walking the miles as we did together every day, walking up the stairway to board a plane, walking up the church steps on Sunday mornings, walking to our boat to go fishing.

How in the world does one calm the emotions when recalling all these precious memories? Ellie and I always thought we would die together. We just knew God would not take one from the other. This should teach us we must never second-guess God. I'm sure He had His own reason for leaving me without my girl. I hope His reason was for me to testify of His love and a lifetime of guidance and mercy for these small-town country kids. No way could we have been kept in the shadows of His smile without His blessing. Love is like that, don'tcha know.

I managed to get out of bed. I pulled the drapes, but no light came into the room; it was the "Darkness of the Dawn" in the life of this special loving couple. I walked through the downstairs of Ellie's beautiful home without purpose. I just walked. I didn't see the love she had placed everywhere: the Spanish vases with flowers, family photos, the hassock that held the afghan and the floor pillows we had used when we slept on the floor by the fireside, her Christmas collection in a corner cabinet, and on the wall her full-length golden mirror that she said was magic because it always made one look good.

I opened the front door, walked out on the porch, and sat where Ellie and I had enjoyed the beautiful sunshine ever since we moved to this lovely home on Lincoln Street. I bit my tongue to hold back the tears as I said out loud, "Darling, you made such a beautiful country place for your Pittman five. You made Lincoln Street a lovely home for you and me. Now, God has taken you to the most beautiful home of all. Thank you, Sweet Jesus, for granting her last request and sending your angels for her in her sleep. I thank you, Lord, that you minimized her suffering and hurts. Oh how sweet are Thy blessings. How sweet to be our lifelong Companion."

Still speaking out loud, I remember saying, "Ellie, darling, I know that after all these years of giving you to me, I know that God will do it one more time. When He opens the Pearly Gates for me, I will see you running across the streets of gold with outstretched arms to me as we did in 1941, when He gave us each other for the very first time. Glory, hallelujah! Amen."

I don't have any idea how long this all took, but I called the hospice nurse, as I had been instructed and was told they would take care of the rest. After doing this, I prepared my angel's face for the undertaker. As I sat and gazed upon my beautiful lady, I told her that angels' wings had whisked her off to heaven in her sleep

118

and that I would love her forever. I whispered, "Thank you, sweetheart, for being the wind beneath my wings all my life."

Now for the really hard part, telling our daughter and sons that their mother had gone to heaven in the night. I prayed that God would help them endure the "Darkness of This Dawn," March 13, 1994.

The family gathered and gazed upon Ellie for the last time on this Earth, and her radiance glowed with the beauty she had always possessed in the flowing of love, kindness, and the caring for others. God blessed her so well, her actions and her life professed, without the title, that she was an Apostle of her Sweet Jesus.

Many words and thoughts ago, I talked to you about a song Ellie and I had written in the seventies. We believed we were composing this song about George Jones and his wife, Tammy, who were getting a divorce; they were Ellie's favorite country stars. Little did we know then, we were writing about our last days together on this Earth. To scribble down these words again just devastates my mind. Darling, if you are listening this moment, in some way tell my heart if, in some mysterious way, you knew our song would be about us? The song is titled "Why in the World."

Why in the world did you make me love you so?
How in the world can I ever let you go?
Why did you put your hand in mine and make your lips taste like
    warm sweet wine?
Now all I have is memories running through my mind.
I search for you in all the places we have been. I hear your
    laughter everywhere.
I can't hide the hurt within even though it's mine to bear.
Sweetheart, the moon the stars
Light nights where you are.
They proclaim my broken heart
Every minute of every day we're apart.
Though I know we'll meet again in our other world
And there you'll still be, my love, my girl,

I just can't help but say,
"Why in the world did you have to go away?"

Wouldn't you know, darling, the beautiful love songs that made us the sweethearts we were would follow us even into death. Oh, how I wish you could kiss away my tears right now and speak to me again the magic words God spilled down into your heart and take away these lonely days and nights that were never supposed to come. How will the "Darkness of the Dawn" ever be lighted again in my heart without you?

9

The days and weeks slowly pass. My children and I do our best to comfort each other with strength God provides from His bountiful mercies.

One day Patricia asked me if we could start a scholarship fund, in her mother's honor, at the high school for seniors who wish to go to college. Don, Roy Mark, and I really got with this idea. Our old school reunion was going to be June 2, 1994, only weeks away. The generosity of family, friends, and neighbors made this project an overwhelming success. The high school principal and Alumni Committee agreed to let me honor Ellie as an outstanding Honor Roll student and the First Drum Corps Major of CJHS. The high school principal accepted an enlarged six-inch-by-twelve-inch photo of Ellie in her Drum Corps uniform. The frame was beautifully done in school colors.

The principal assured the alumni that a special place would be forthcoming for this special addition to the school's archives. Roy Mark presented this treasure, which was accepted with honor. Patricia then stepped to the podium and presented the Alumni Committee with over $3,000 in scholarship funds, which was the largest single amount donated to this cause since its inception. What an honor for such a deserving lady.

As our meeting adjourned, I wanted to be alone with my thoughts, which went back to Grandma Lilly, Ellie's mother. Many times, when I had been working near her home, I stopped by for a visit on the porch. We often talked about honoring Ellie at school events, but my girl had always refused because she thought it would be embarrassing. I can just hear Grandma Lilly's voice now, saying, "C.E., we finally did it. I just knew your love for my daughter would

121

be forever." In my heart, I respond, *God saw to that. Love is like that don'tcha know.*

Our local daily paper was fortunate to have a very capable writer, named Mary Guccione, who through kindness set up the possibility of Ellie having a special honor day at an all-school assembly so we could present her Drum Corps picture. Mary had arranged this with the principal some while back. Ellie's stroke, however, had made this impossible.

Even as it was, we would have taken Ellie in a wheelchair; we would have been the *mature* Pittman five. I would have been so proud and honored to show off my beautiful lady one more time. But it just wasn't meant to be.

So as I was alone with my thoughts, I had to be so thankful for this wonderful day at the place where Ellie and I had first met so long ago.

Soon after, neighbors and friends just poured out their hearts to me. The twins' mother, H.J., prepared a whole birthday dinner, including turkey, cake, and all, for me. In lieu of a potted flower or sprays, they gave me a live dogwood tree. With H.J., another friendship of great joy had grown between the five of us.

H.J. and the twins, Russ and Mitch, were caring enough to put on this lovely birthday dinner. There was enough to have a party, and I'm sure that was their intention. But I didn't have enough sense about me at the time to realize it, and I have been too embarrassed to inquire about it ever since. Forgiven? OK! Thanks.

I also owe thanks to our neighbors Don and Dixie, and Christine and her four children. God never has a chance to sleep, as He is constantly watching out for me.

I was also fortunate for dear friends like W.J. and Lois, who always put some joy back in my heart when they would visit, which was often.

Dixie's mother, Polly Raye, wrote a poem, and the following is her thoughts of me and Ellie.

True Love Forever

Your love, she has gone to dwell
In a beautiful place, with her Heavenly Father
Who has already welcomed her
Through his pearly gates.
She will look down, watch and say
To you, her love,
"I'm at rest and I'm at peace.
No more hurts, no more pain,
Everything is beautiful.
All my days remain the same,
So I thank you, my sweetheart,
For the tender loving care you gave
While on this Earth I stayed.
So in our memory, I will always be your first love
For you will never know, how much you meant to me.
So good night, my love!
Forever now I will sleep in peace,
For all my pain has been released.
In God's Hands, I now rest.
Just to be with God, I'm truly Blessed.
So, my friend, it's not the end
For someday you two will meet again."

It is early summer 1995, now, and it seems there is no escape
from the sadness of the spring of 1994. The "Darkness of the Dawn"
would not let up even in the sunshine days of April and May. I tried
to find solace at our houseboat, which was so much a part of Ellie's
and my life, but to no avail.

I find the only peace of mind is in doing and completing the
things Ellie and I had planned together. One such project was to
cover the patio by the rose garden, which she enjoyed so much. This
would allow it to be used in any kind of weather. We had planned

123

on being able to enjoy breakfast and coffee there on any morning we wanted.

I finished the project today and sat sipping my coffee and looking out the window. I saw a couple of bluebirds making a nest in a house we had offered them, for free, a couple of years ago. We didn't think they were ever going to come.

I continued sipping my coffee, which was beginning to get cold, and my heart told me, *C.E., God isn't going to leave you alone. Don't you know He has counted your every tear? He even knows how many sleepless nights and all the torment that's in you. He knows that sometimes the bitterness rears its ugly head when you are suffering the most. Old boy, just keep on listening to your heart and soul, and you'll find He still has His Open Hand reaching out to you in hopes you'll put yours back into His again, so the two of you can walk together as before. God never gives up on us. It is always me who gives up on Him. Praises and praises that He is always willing to take us back again.*

Still thinking on these thoughts, I walked around our lawn, looking for signs of life in our shrubbery after the cold winter months.

One day, about two years ago, Ellie and I were paddling upriver in our paddleboat and fishing. She spotted a pretty little red berry tree on the bank. It was about five or six feet tall. She exclaimed, "I sure would like to have that pretty tree! Do you think we could dig it up to take home?"

Well, you're right; we dug it up and planted it at the corner of the summer house. After almost two years, it still showed no signs of those pretty little red berries. Ellie said, "C.E., do you think you got the right tree?"

Oh Lord, how I wish for you today, my love, because as I approached the little tree of ours I saw that it had small green berries, which will turn red in the summer. These were the berries we thought would never come.

I couldn't help looking up into heaven and saying out loud, "See, Ellie, I didn't dig up the wrong tree. See the berries?"

I was so amazed. God, again, was helping me to feel the closeness of my girl as though I could almost feel her touch. Love is like that, don'tcha know.

Our next-door neighbor's deck was only about twenty feet or so from this cute little tree, and as I turned around I could see she was going into her house. One can imagine what thoughts were going around in her mind when she heard me talking out loud, probably: *He's going crazy.*

However, little did she know that God and Ellie and I were just talking about life's blessing in a little red berry tree.

As the summer progressed, the red berries were but another prize for two young lovers, because no other home in our town would have a cute little tree with the reddest berries for our birds to feast on during the winter months. Speaking of winter, except for the three years of World War II, this past Christmas was the only Christmas I didn't purchase a gift. I made several attempts to find something at the North Park Mall, but the hurt was just too great. I asked my family to omit gifts this year and I would give to our charity the amount their mother and I would normally spend for gifts, which gave me a little satisfaction.

At the kettle for the bell ringers on the street, I turned back to look at this person who was giving his time freely so someone else could have a special Christmas. All the way home I couldn't shake this sight. I put my purchases away and put a box of candy on the dining room table so I could share it with guests who would drop in. The light finally came on in my brain. I jumped back into the car and went back to the store and purchased another box of candy. As I was going to my car, I gave this box of candy to the bell ringer and said, "Merry Christmas, and thank you." His surprised look prompted me to do this at other locations. Isn't love fun?

Every day now, I could see families, sweethearts, and friends having the best time preparing for the holidays, and the hurt so deep inside my being would not cease. I made a special effort to hide myself and my grief from neighbors, family, and friends, until I awakened one morning about 2:30 A.M. and couldn't go back to sleep. I just lay there, thinking of how much joy Ellie and I always had making things ready for this very special, happy season. I could almost smell the Christmas fruit and nut candies that were so festive with all the spices, dates, pecans, and raisins. I jumped out of bed, put on my robe, and hustled into the kitchen in search of that cookie recipe. This was about December 15, and I found in Ellie's recipe boxes the cure for my aching heart.

By the time Christmas Eve came, I had baked 1,500 cookies and delivered them all. I hoped that all recipients would accept them as my small way to say "thank you" for all the love through the last awful, cruel year. I surely found unexpected joy in doing this because, while flipping through Ellie's recipe boxes, I found poems, love notes, and Bible verses mingled around and through her recipe cards. Some were heartbreaking, like the notes I had clipped to her haircut money and tips.

One such note was this: "Thank you, my sweet barber." And on the other side, Ellie had written: "I love you, C.E."

Sometimes I had tried to make little poems, which is stretching the imagination. One of them was: "Please accept my Christmas tips, because you're about the best that clips. Love, C.E." We always got a good laugh from my efforts. At the bottom of this poem, as always, Ellie had written: "I love you, C.E."

Another note I had written read: "An extra tip to attest you are always a cut above the rest. C.E." I never ever got tired of the note at the bottom: "I love you, C.E."

Ellie really was a good barber. She only used a comb, scissors, and a double-edged grooming razor. Her ability didn't require clippers and all the other barber tools. Of course, all the hugs and kisses, after being dusted off, were something that barbershops didn't offer. Ellie would always cut my hair on the deck of our winter Texas condo, and as people would stare at times, she would say to me, "C.E., does this embarrass you?" My reply was always: "They're just jealous because they don't have a beautiful barber like I do." Love is like that, don'tcha know.

I'm sure by now you can imagine the feeling within me when it's time to go to the barbershop downtown. But, then again, who was ever as lucky as me? Thank you, Sweet Jesus.

As I go to the Old 66 Highway Barber Shop, in the Royal Heights subdivision of Joplin, I pass by our old schooldays dance place called Cottage Inn, and for twenty or thirty blocks my mind is filled with happy memories of that long hardwood dance floor. It was there Ellie and I really learned to dance together on Saturday nights.

The beautiful songs from a large old nickelodeon just seemed to play so our hearts could fall deeper in love, songs like "The Way You Look Tonight," "Careless," "In Other Words," "Stardust," "Old Black Magic," "Deep Purple," "Near You," "Remember Me," "They Can't Take That Away from Me," "Smoke Gets in Your Eyes," "Portrait of My Love," "Fascination," "Can't Remember When," "Yours," "If Ever I Should Leave You," "September Song," "You'll Never Know (Just How Much I Miss You)," "Falling Leaves," "All The Things You Are," "String of Pearls," "Have I Told You Lately," "Two Sleepy People," "Till," "The Nearness of You," "Once in a While," "Harbor Lights," "On the Street Where You Live," "It's All in the Game," "Impossible," "The Impossible Dream," and "Where or When."

Every beautiful song had its own meaning and thrill in the hearts of Ellie and me. One just can't have his sweetheart in a tender embrace, dancing on the clouds of these beautiful melodies, searching the depths of her eyes, and not fall in love. Our secret, beyond this point, was that we took the hands we held right than and reached out to the open hand of God so the three of us walked through this world together. Hallelujah! Amen.

Surely that's the way love grows, don'tcha know.

Ellie girl, to write the following words are a must: Did you know you were my heroine and you are all things I ever wanted to be? Did you know that I would be nothing without you? With you I can fly as high as an eagle flies because you are the wind beneath my wings. I shall always hear the wings of an eagle when the summer breezes filter though the trees. I will always hear your loving voice, saying, "Oh no, C.E., you are my hero because I said it first!"

No wonder Ellie would cut out beautiful poems and put them in her little special drawer in the hallway table, poems like "In My Heart," from *Portraits,* by John C. Metcalf.

In "In My Heart," the author creates a feeling from the young years to the older years in the lives of two lovers.

It just seems to be written for Ellie and me because we never got old to each other, either. Ellie's beauty and gracefulness was timeless. Her soft whisper, "I love you, C.E.," was just precious when she sealed it with a tender kiss. My aging eyes can only see Ellie as my beautiful lady, my love, my life.

At the top of this clipping, Ellie had written in ink: "To my C.E." Now, that's how true love is, don'tcha know.

Aren't poems like songs? They just seem to fuel a loving energy between sweethearts.

A love song, heard in early morning, will cause one to hum it all day long. It just will not go away. A poem like "In My Heart," read early in the day, will cause one's mind to keep a precious thought for hours and, more times than not, cause one to shop on the way home from work for a special little gift for the one he loves. How such a small effort can master a whole evening of such great joy between two people is a miracle. One could think that's where the saying "tender loving care" originated. It helps us kindle the flames of love and prevents the smoke of indifference from quenching the warmth of a loving feeling. Isn't being in love a fun way to live one's lifetime? It's heartbreaking that this saying could not be directed to everyone.

As I continued to walk through our Lincoln Street yard, in

search of early signs of spring, there was still evidence of an eight-inch snow from a few days before. It was Ellie's kind of snow, which hung on the tree limbs and put snow caps on everything it fell upon.

When I awoke on the first morning of the snow to an incredible land of beauty, I just had to take Ellie's photo to the window and show her that I had not forgotten her joy at this sight and bless the handiwork of God.

I kicked over a little mound of roses by the flagpole, and to my surprise some little sprigs of grape hyacinths were emerging from their winter hiding place. As I stooped over to touch them, the brisk south breeze caused Old Glory to snap her colors as if to say, as Ellie often had, "Thank you, C.E., for doing your part to allow this peaceful kind of day."

The urge to reach out and take Ellie by the hand to walk with me through the day was so strong. I walked a step or two with an outstretched arm and didn't even realize it. Crocus buds were pushing their little heads through the ground, and the first flowers of spring turned my mind to the swiftly approaching Valentine's Day. That would be the day I'd make believe my sweetheart was here, and I would kiss the rose I put into her lovely hand and listen as she said, "C.E., our roses are so beautiful this morning." I would enjoy a cup of her special coffee and reminisce of the times that brought us to this moment, a time only God could have planned and made as perfect as Himself.

My dear, sweet friends still shower me with their caring affection. Lois and I still go shopping and share lunch together several times a month. Mitch, Russ, and H.J. are always picking me up when I'm down. Today I was invited to their roller-skating party and a Pizza Inn lunch. I told you, some time ago, that God wasn't going to leave me alone. Can't you see His love is like that, don'tcha know.

Jesus tells us, in chapter 5 of Matthew, that "we are the salt of the earth. We are the light of the world and we should let our light shine before men that they might see the good works and glorify Our Father which is heaven." In some small, magical way, I hope the life he gave freely to Ellie and me can be our light to shine before men and profess God's love for such earthlings of no significance except to Him. So we take heed not to do alms before men but to glorify Our Father who is in heaven; that is our daily prayer. I have faith and trust He will multiply our words of love and praise for Him and feed the souls who read these words as He multiplied the fishes and the bread for the multitude so that their hunger was filled.

The essence of what I hope to proclaim is Matthew 10:32. When Jesus was talking to his disciples, He said, "Whosoever therefore shall confess me before men, him I will confess also before my Father which is in heaven." And this is where my sweetheart Ellie would say, "Thank you, Sweet Jesus."

We must be ever vigilant, because Jesus is coming soon. We also must remember Jesus said, "For by our words we shall be justified and by our words we shall be condemned." We truly hope and pray he will look upon all our efforts and find them justifiable in his sight. I know of no others so richly blessed as Ellie and me, and I hope our efforts in this writing will find his favor. Amen.

While at church today, I could hardly keep my attention on the lesson in John chapter 6, of the little boy with loaves and two fishes and the miracle of Jesus feeding thousands with this meager amount. Remember, a few words ago, when I hoped God would use this book as a blessing to all who read it in hopes He would multiply these words in their hearts as He did the loaves and fishes and the readers would take His hand and walk through this world?

Many times, as I have endeavored to justify our faith and beliefs with words from the Holy Book, invariably these thoughts would be spoken by our minister, Randy Gariss, who was our capable teacher Sunday after Sunday. God surely works in His own way.

10

Today being the last Monday in January 1995, I'm cleaning house, dusting, vacuuming, changing linens, washing dirty clothes, etc. Ellie always marked this day on the calendar as a reminder, and I have followed her procedures for almost a year now. I still make believe she is helping me to turn the king-size mattress. I don't know if this feeling will ever go away. If ever it does, I know I will miss it, because in some ways it's a comfort to me, if only in my heart and mind. God only knows how very much I love this girl. We were each other's bright evening star.

At the first signs of twilight, it seemed as though our energy became boundless and we were always ready for whatever the night would offer. Just being together after a day's work would assure us that happiness and joy would reign whatever the darkness would bring, like going to Little League baseball games, shopping for family needs, visiting with family members or friends, having a candlelight dinner out and dancing the night away, clearing trees off the land at our country place and splitting them for a split-rail fence, making a large bonfire of the tree trimmings that could be seen for miles in the darkness of the night. Before calling it quits, as the fire burned down, we roasted wieners and marshmallows, because the evening work had whet our appetites.

On one such occasion, as we watched our fire dwindle to a safe stage, Ellie screamed and jumped into my arms with her feet off the ground. She yelled, "It's a snake!" I could see this curious critter was a blacksnake, which only wanted to examine our fire or just curl up in its warmth and go to sleep. I carried Ellie to the driveway where she felt safe. Sweet life and precious memories, oh, how they do linger.

Later, we said our prayers, as always, and kissed goodnight, and I searched for Ellie's hand and snuggled down for a good night's sleep while wishing for the night to swiftly pass so God could grant Ellie and me another day together. That's how love was with Ellie and me, don'tcha know.

While my mind and heart are still in a memory stage, I can see my Ellie sitting on our rail fence, which we made together, with her kitty, Jerry, a pretty steel gray cat. He just loved it when Ellie would let him sit on her shoulder with his tail wagging down her back. What a cute picture this is in my mind today.

I say to myself when every new morning arrives, "Please, Lord, help me to lift the 'Darkness of the Dawn' today so I can clearly see Your path, which You want me to walk." It always seems to point to this writing to pay tribute and honor to my very special lady and my small way to glorify God to the men and women who are reading this book about two real American country kids whom God blessed with His special kind of love for a lifetime.

It's been over a year now since the first word was penned in the effort to write this book, and along the way, many times, the author has been told, "You must pick a subject like the filth of today's world of sex to have a reading audience." Well, you see, they who gave out this advice just don't have the faith in God's words when He said, "I will not forsake thee. I am your God and you are My People." His love will prevail. To have a positive effect on the lives of young people, who are starting a new life together as man and wife, is the desired blessing for this author. To share one's private life with the world is like walking the streets naked with no place to hide, if you don't know God.

Over these many months, when contemplating another sentence, I could almost feel a power pushing the pen in my hand to express the desired thought. Now, if that isn't a heavenly intervention then I'm at a loss as to its identity. There are but a few paragraphs left in this love story about these small-town kids, Ellie and C.E., though I can still feel the magic Ellie put into my life. Love is like that, don'tcha know.

When God gives you an angel from His heaven, to be an angel in your life forever, God Almighty, how great Thou really art.

It is always difficult to understand why some, in one's life, are more loving than others. Our first grandchild, Cindy, was one such loving girl, who always loved Ellie. When Cindy and Mike, her husband, moved to Texas she always, without fail, sent a monthly note to her grandma. Since Ellie's demise, Cindy has visited me several times, and every visit, for five or six days, was just lovely.

Cindy is so much like Ellie and me. After Ellie's death, Cindy would call me and ask, "Grandpa, can we get some Michelob and go fishing?" Of course, I was always thrilled and said, "We sure can."

Sometimes we fished and sometimes we got rained out. On rainy days we'd just order pizza and sit by the fire. Often she would say, "Come on, Grandpa; let's dance." And we'd go to the kitchen and dance as Ellie and I used to do. Like us, Cindy is sensible and enjoys life. She was very close to us. Both before and after Ellie's passing, not very long a time went by but a card was in the mail from this precious young lady.

Today, I received the cutest friendship card from her and you can see she is certainly a part of Ellie and me. On the front of the card are musical notes and staffs and these words: "Friendship is like music"; and on the inside it reads: "Some high notes, some low notes, but always a wonderful song. Love, Cindy and Mike."

Thank you, girl!

I always enjoy telling my friends, when they are so nice to me, that God has a very large Book and in His hand is a golden pen; every time you are so good, like this, He writes down your name and that's how you are rewarded in heaven. And Cindy, girl, you are no exception. Love just makes nice people nicer. That was the way of my Ellie.

If I had to choose one day to be my life forever, I would choose the morning we left Hawaii on our first trip. When our plane gained altitude for our flight, our seat belts were off and the music of "Impossible Dream" was floating into our cabin. The tenderness and sweetness that Ellie showed to me, by kissing my finger as I led her gently to the aisle so we could dance so closely; smiling through our tears! The love that just seemed to sweep us off our feet, at thirty thousand feet above the sea, made this one of the most precious moments of my life. No wonder we always loved to dance to the songs "Beyond the Sea" and, of course, our "Impossible Dream." It was our life.

Ellie, the memory of these very special moments with you just fill my heart with love that will never end. As my eyes fill with a million tears without you, I have no way to turn them off. For almost a year, now, I have come to your resting place every day with roses that occupy the place in my hand where your hand always was. We seem to have spiritual words together with God as always, and as I leave to go home the feeling in my heart is so good, like going home from Sunday church. That's when we always said, "Lord help us to be more like Thee this week than last."

Sweetheart, you would love this winter on Lincoln Street; it has been almost like spring ever since December.

This morning, as I went to make coffee, I looked at the out-of-doors temperature; it was forty degrees at eight o'clock. I said, "Happy February 1, sweetheart; we're going to have coffee on the patio." And we did. Most people would say I was crazy. But, to me, you are so real. Love is like that, don'tcha know.

By noon the temperature was up to almost seventy. If you were here we would have been off to the houseboat and, as usual, you would catch more black bass or crappie than me. I had new carpet put in our boat and the upholstery company made us a boat flag that states: "STAR ONE." That's you, sweetheart; you have been my number-one star for a lifetime, and I'm still awed by this lifetime of beauty that was ours.

After almost every September now, I hear myself saying,

"Ellie, darling, why in the world did you have to go away? Why did you put your hand in mine so many years ago?"

By this time, dear, you are saying, "C.E., that's the way true love is! Don'tcha know?"

Yes, Ellie, I do. And do you remember how you would try so hard to be the first to find bluebells and cowslips in the spring? This always began in the middle to late March. But this year, Patricia and I found them, and also buttercups, in February. You would be so excited. The fire bush and baby's breath are also blooming this early. Sweetheart, you were always younger than springtime and more beautiful than all the flowers.

Speaking of flowers and February, I saw a recipe for a Toll House cookie Valentine heart that I can make from scratch in your heart-shaped cake tin. It sure looked cute and I'm going to try it if I can locate your cake pan. I have looked two or three times, without success, for your pan. So please talk to me in my sleep. If you will, I shall try my hand at this beauty after church tomorrow. I'll even save a piece for you and me to have with our Monday morning coffee.

Gee, how sweet the first cup of coffee was every morning with you. Darling, do you really know how very much I have loved you? And do you see how very much I miss you? I have not called you by the name Sweet Tata (like Sweet Potato) because I was afraid you might scold me for divulging this in public. But now I've done it, and maybe, if this writing is successful, the whole world will know that my angel from God at times was called this endearing name, Sweet Tata. You live in heaven now, and that's got to be a first. OK, Sweet Tata?

I can just see your precious smile, which many people say was your trademark.

Sweetheart, I met two very dear old friends at the post office today. You remember Art Simpson, who was a frequent customer at the Pittmans' Chicken Inn. The other fiend was the Man with the Golden Trumpet, a professional horn man at Hidden Acres supper club for many years. Remember? He always called me Uncle Cec, which I could never understand, but I always felt these were endearing words. Mr. Bill Pearson's music entertained our dancing feet to the applause of the band, dinner guests, and waitresses alike with songs like "Mac the Knife," "Smoke Gets in Your Eyes," and even a tango or cha-cha tune to break the slow pace of the slower tunes. Bill's wife was in heaven almost a month before you.

Bill asked me if I still talked to you, and I said, "Sure. And I even dance with her in the kitchen. I even kiss her picture every morning and at night before bedtime. I still hold her hand in my every prayer and search for that special touch in the dark of night. That's the way love holds on, don'tcha know."

Sweetheart, I potted the tulip bulbs that you thought were so pretty last March. I put them on the windowsill in our master bedroom and today they are beginning to show buds. When they're in full bloom, I will bring them to your resting place in hopes you can enjoy them again.

Your children bring flowers almost every week, and Roy Mark brings fresh roses even on cold winter days. I'm sure he knows they will freeze in night temperatures, but that's his love he's putting there, not the roses. I'm sure that makes you feel very happy to know. Your family might only be the Pittman four now, but oh, we still love you, Ellie darling.

How sweet it is for me to see family love still thriving during the sadness of your absence. This is what seems to make the human race work: obedience to family values, obedience to God's word, obedience to parents, and obedience to marriage vows. Can't you see all of the above put into play at once? I think it would shock this world to pieces.

It seems when we commit to whatever, it takes obedience to make it work. Just look at divorce, crime, and family troubles. This love triangle, God, Ellie, and me makes three, will encourage better family relations by people honoring mother and father and their loving their children. This, I'm sure, would create a resurgence of moral standards and the teaching of same in the home, so our schools and churches would have something to begin with when first-graders start. I know it seems so hard to begin. The only way I can tell you is by experience.

Jesus holds out his hand to us even while walking on the water. He still holds out his hand while he stills the water. Just take hold of what he offers and walk with him—you'll find that nothing is impossible with Jesus.

This love story, or impossible dream, could not have come true without Ellie and me doing this very thing. At this moment, she is saying, "Thank you, Sweet Jesus, for being a part of our love triangle. You not only made our life together work, but You made it a happy life forever."

I hope you all will remember the key words are obedience and love.

Ellie, this is Valentine's Day, 1995. Do you remember the Valentine card you gave me last year? You told me, by its verse, I was your music and when I wasn't present the music just played on in your mind like an old love song. You always knew the sweetest words to say to my heart. Every day since you've been gone, I can still hear these sweet sayings, just as if you were so close I could touch you. I guess the writer who penned "I Can't Stop Loving You" knew about us.

As our children and I place fresh flowers, including roses, in your hands today, I hope you know we will all love you forever and ever.

It reminds me of the time on Mother's Day when you and I gave my mother, Susie Alice, flowers and she said to us, "It's so nice to have the gift of flowers while one can still smell their beauty."

The flowers we brought you today will freeze on this winter's night, I'm sure. But the love from whence they came will never fade as will the petals of the roses tomorrow.

This past year, our children and I have read to you almost daily

137

from *God's Little Prayer Book* when we sat on the cement bench that was placed by your resting place. I can see that God is gradually helping them to control their hurts and sadness. You would be so proud of them. I know if they will just keep in touch with God, they can make it on their own now. Maybe I can, too, especially when the thought of you catches up with me.

Sweetheart, some pages ago I told you that this winter has been so very mild, like seventy degrees in the first part of February. However, the last few days winter has returned and I keep hearing a little voice inside me, as I did when you were here, say, *Ask Ellie about Corpus Christi today and leave the snow and cold behind.* I can always hear us toting our groceries up the metal stairway on Friday afternoons. You would be so embarrassed when we reached the landing and some of the guests would look out their door because I had clogged my western boots so loud on the metal steps. Then, to make it worse, I would act like the two very, very heavy grocery sacks made me do it. Once inside our condo, I fell on the floor, bags and all, and just died laughing. Remember your remark? "C.E., I'm going to the office for our mail and report you to the management!"

As you turned toward the door you just stopped still and then turned around and looked at me on the floor and gently lay down beside me. I'm sure if the perturbed neighbors could have seen us, they would have been so envious, as they showed very little affection for each other.

As soon as you were out of sight, I called and asked for George, who was a very friendly employee, and told him what to say to you when he gave you our mail. You came back and told me what he said. I couldn't keep it from you, so I explained while we put away our food in the kitchen. I made one mistake, and that was telling you when the kitchen faucet was in reach. Gee! Did you ever soak me with the spray hose! Oh well, it was Friday and bath night anyway. (At least that's what everyone thinks of country boys: a

Friday or Saturday bath schedule.) Darling, you were so much fun, and sometimes I was too much of a tease. Maybe?

Oh, darling Ellie, you have made the world go away a zillion times in your own special way. That's how love grows—two hearts together, one love forever. You were my lady, my love, my wife, my friend, and my life. For that I shall always cherish the memory of you, as the beautiful, elegant lady we knew as Ellie.

Ellie, do you remember when we were at the marina, which was busy with shrimp boats, and a guy landed a pontoon plane right by us? He got out on the wharf and asked us for a smoke. He had unlawfully landed on that stretch of water, so he asked if the Corpus Christi patrol was tough. Not knowing what he was up to, we said yes. When he began to hike out of there, we had the gall to ask him to take our picture. To our surprise he took our camera and did just that and then took off with the sea water just splashing away. Even though he was in the wrong, somehow, we hoped he would get off free.

All of this happened on a Friday. We then walked about a block to one of our favorite places: the floating restaurant with three or four dining rooms and lounges. The seafood was superb, and dancing with my girl was even more enjoyable. By this time, darkness had swallowed up the sunshine on the bay. We went on our way to Cal Allen, a subdivision community where we loved to dance to boats scooting and "Cotton-Eyed Joe."

Ellie, darling, life with you surely didn't know the word *boring*. Now it's hard to believe the question a country song title asks whether or not if the good life is over? All I know is there will never be good times like you and I have known. That's why memories are so important. At least no one can take those precious times away from us. I wish right now that I could show you how much I love you for all of them.

When we first started this beautiful life together in Pueblo, trying to live on sixteen dollars a week and owning little, no car, no furniture, and few clothes, we had each other as our prize possessions. Little did we dream that so very many of God's beautiful creations would be made available to us. I daresay few have enjoyed them to the extent that we did. Who else could spill a glob of ice cream on his new aloha shirt while sitting on a banyan tree root having lunch at a bus stop and not get upset? Or being abandoned by Aloha Air Lines on the leper island of Molokai? We were the only couple who visited this island that day. There was only one eating place and one rental car place; I don't know if there was a motel or not. It didn't seem to bother us much. We just explored Ginger Gardens while the airline sent a special plane for us. They gave us leis and free dinners on our arrival in Honolulu. Boy!, Sweetheart, we were something special that night; they just couldn't quit being nice to us.

Memories of days gone by, how beautiful they were and so were you, Ellie. I could live them all over again and with you they would be brand new. I really know you could do the same with me because your beautiful eyes have told me so, over and over again. That's the way love grows, don'tcha know?

How exciting you made every moment.

Ellie, darling, now that my life has bloomed its peak and the petals have turned from red to brown like a rose from your garden, I must tell you that when I was so very young I asked God for you, for an angel from heaven. Oh, what joy when He opened our eyes to each other on the first day of school in 1937. Every day since, when our eyes opened to each other in the morning, it was like seeing you for the first time all over again. I never knew that the coming fifty years would be like a miracle every day. Our life together was like a dream; sometimes it was so unbelievable, even to me, how we, together, could turn a seeming defeat into a victory, a tear into a smile, a heartache into laughter, or bad times into good times. As we grew from teens to adults, we talked on these things so many times and gradually understood that God doesn't take you under His wing without giving you some kind of power to cope with any situation. We began to know that was the way He made love grow.

I never realized, when I wanted God to send me an angel like you, that you would also possess the magic to make my heart to fall in love with you every day just like new. He gave you the magic to bear our three beautiful children and be the strength for the Pittman five, to nurture our lives along the way, to embrace each of us as if it were going to be the last hug for life. I just knew your hurts when, at times, the ones so close to you only responded half-heartedly. If only they had known, as I did, that an embrace can speak words of love but not utter a sound. Every human being should know God is the author of love, for God *is* love. He is pleased to see us share this bountiful blessing. I do not think there is a stronger word in God's book than the word *love*.

Getting back to today's events, the winter flu bug is going around this month and I steered clear of it until yesterday. I had to get a drink of water during church to stop my cough. Today, I'm all stopped up, like we were in Texas several winters ago. I surely hope this time isn't as bad.

My fiends H.J., Russ, and Mitch came to my rescue again with chicken noodle soup. Russ wanted me to pick him up so badly, but I told him I didn't want him to get my cold, so he just hugged my leg. Isn't that cute for a four-year-old boy?

The twins will be five March 31. They don't have any little boys their age on our block, so I'm going to ask H.J. if I can teach them to play baseball so when they're six they can be Little League players with some experience.

Ellie, I wish you were here to help us. You would love the fun because you are such a big baseball fan. I thought of you many times last fall when there was a baseball strike and no World Series. They still have not solved their problems yet, and here 1995 spring training is upon us. Baseball is no different than every venture in today's world: money, money, money.

Sweetheart, I'm happy to say the monetary aspect of this

writing wasn't intended to be of the same nature as O.J.'s and Speaker Newt's. On the contrary, the purpose was, and is, to honor a most precious lady named Ellie and to profess God's living presence with us, which caused us to radiate our love of a lifetime to everyone who knew us.

Even stronger, Ellie darling, I thank you again for making the world go away so many times, so love could grow. It was like pulling the weeds from a strawberry patch so the little green berries could nature into the reddest, ripest, and sweetest.

I thank you for having faith in me when it seemed you stood alone. Thank you for a million happy moments and memories that seemed to take us to the moon. Angel face, thank you for all the moments in the stillness of the night with the stars and the moon; for the brightness of the sun on a lovely afternoon; for the wind and rain upon your pretty face; and for the piece of heaven in your embrace. These times were my riches and my success. Thank you, darling, for making them mine. They are the golden moments of my lifetime.

Did I forget to tell you that you were my idol? Don'tcha know I would have not been much without you. You being so-so, I wanted to be just like you. With you I found my strength and my sanity. I could have ascended easily to the white, fluffy clouds of the Missouri summertime skies. Isn't that nice to know now after all these years!

Oh, how wisdom comes so late in life, when it is so desperately needed in the younger years. These times seem to be a struggle to know which way to turn and which path to walk. Just walk through life with God, and He will point you in the right direction always. He assures success every time.

Ellie darling, whatever gains I have conquered in this world, which most people would define as success, that has not been the motivation of my being. The only success I claim is my true and faithful love for you, as we found the magic of holding hands and its motivation in the lives of sweethearts like us. The only time this country boy will flaunt success is when my numbered days have been exhausted and I still have the strength and power of this rugged guy, which I have always been, to reach up to heaven and hold so gently and tenderly your hands in mine. Together again, we will place them into the open hand of God, as always, and the three of us will walk through the gates of heaven together. This will be the very last time God will ever have to give you back to me. True love is like that, don'tcha know. And I'm sure you do by now!

Until that day, darling, I hope you will pray that God will give me the right to hold you ever so tight and to feel the nearness of you in the night. From the Fox Farm west of Carl Junction to the mining chat piles of Oronogo, from the first day I ever saw you at school when you were only fifteen years old, it was you who made our life such a beautiful journey through this world. It seems you were so correct when you always told me that you wanted to leave this world first because you would not be able to cope with all the memories and photos of the past. Darling, in some ways this is true, but again, I have found in this past year that these are such unusual memories that they have their own way to stay the sadness and lighten the load.

However, when twilight comes every evening and the Fridays and Saturdays with their restlessness, it's so hard to cope, which leaves me alone with my tears. I wonder where all these tears come from. By now, you and I could have had our own river from the ones I have shed, most of which were happy ones.

Sweetheart, February has come and gone and here we are at March 13, 1995. On this day last year, you were whisked away to heaven on angel wings and I wasn't sure I could ever last another year without you. I guess the thought of you and your spirit just keeps me hanging on. God promised He would not leave me alone, and He surely has kept His promise on my behalf. You are still like the woman in the Bobby Goldsboro song titled "Honey," because you still seem to be here so many times in the days and nights. It's where love and laughter was always present, not just in our home

143

but especially in my heart, where you will always stay! True love is like that, don'tcha know!

I'm sure forever could not change the way we were. Every day I'm prayerful and thankful for you and that in some way God will let you know you were my first love and will always be my last true love. I have no other way to express my loneliness without you except to say it hurts like hell. I just don't think it will ever change until I see you again.

I pray to God he will help me to finish this book, and today He has blessed me with that wish because in just minutes that will be accomplished. I hope you approve of all the things I have said in written words. I didn't know, at the beginning over a year ago, that I would have varying thoughts about revealing our lives to the world. In some ways, I'm sorry to see the end. It made me feel so close to you, but if our story will help the couples of the world to fall in love as we did, then it's our blessing as well as theirs. God will see to that, don'tcha know.

When two are truly in love, the actions of their nearness are not governed by the crowds of the world. It seems lovers are in a world of their own, without spectators. The only sounds they hear are the violins and the music being played heart to heart. This is serenity in the lifetime of man and wife.

I'll be seeing you around our home and watching you pluck the roses from our garden. I'll hear your laughter and feel your love upon my lips and the very warmth of your nearness to me.

It kept us at the top of the world and taught us to go hand in hand, dancing through white, fluffy clouds of summer skies and leaving shadows in the moonlight; so many times I could not count. These times were loving, thrilling, and beautiful just as you'll always be to me. Life, what an exciting experience with my lady. It just went so fast, we had such little time to love. Thank you, sweet Jesus, for the precious time you gave to Ellie and me.

God bless the young lovers of the world, that they might find the true happiness You showered upon Ellie and me.

Sweetheart, I know we'll meet again in our other world, and there you'll still be my love, my girl. Glory Hallelujah! Heaven is like that, don'tcha know?

Amen and amen.